The Concept of Niyāma in Buddhism.

Other Books by Jayarava

Pilgrimage Diary
Nāmapada: A Guide to Names in the Triratna Buddhist Order
Visible Mantra: Visualising and Writing Buddhist Mantras
Talking to the Kālāmas
Karma and Rebirth Reconsidered

Available from: https://www.lulu.com/spotlight/VisibleMantraPress

Websites

www.visiblemantra.org
jayarava.org
jayarava.blogspot.com

The Concept of Niyāma in Buddhism: Source Texts & Interpretations

Jayarava

Visible Mantra Press
2021

Copyright © Jayarava, 2021. The author has asserted his moral right to be identified as the author of this work. All rights reserved.

ISBN 978-0-9566929-3-1

Published by

Visible Mantra Press
2 Shelly Row
CB3 0BP
United Kingdom
visiblemantra@gmail.com

In Memory of Sangharakshita
(1925-2018)

"Resolved fearlessly to pursue, frankly to examine and faithfully to accept and follow whatever the truth about Buddhism might turn out to be"
(*A Survey of Buddhism*. 7th Ed. 1993, p38)

Contents

Preface

These translations were produced in 2012 with the *Triratna Buddhist Order* and the *Triratna Buddhist Community* in mind. I have been slow to publish them mainly because other concerns seem more important, but I never lost interest in *niyāma* as a concept. The essays that follow date from 2014 – 2020. These are not easy texts to translate, a combination of the dense commentarial idiom and recondite Abhidhamma jargon makes them quite esoteric. The Pāli commentaries are a literary, rather than an oral genre; written by and for members of an educated elite who often possessed a knowledge of the Sanskrit language and Classical Indian literature. They make much greater use of the agglutinating character of Pāli, constructing long, elaborate compounds that leave the uninitiated to puzzle over the implied grammatical relationships.

However, the texts can almost always be comprehended with some effort. Where I remain unsure of a reading, I have indicated this in footnotes. Those interested in Abhidhamma terminology might like to consult Bodhi's (1993) translation of the *Abhidhammattha Saṅgaha*, a Theravāda Abhidhamma training manual, for more information.

A translator is generally constrained to choose a single translation for key terms, but the reader should be aware that the alternative connotations would have been obvious to the intended audience and that they need to be kept in mind. The choice of translations is not unlimited, but neither does the translator's choice constrain the word to mean only one thing in the target language. Equally, the English speaking reader must be cautious about applying the broad range of English connotations to the translated word and must try to keep in mind that the author of the text lived centuries ago in India or Sri Lanka. Ideally, someone who cannot read the original should always consult more than one translation but in the meantime, they must read these (and all) translations with a critical eye.

These texts represent three periods in history and three different cultures. The *suttas* were originally an Iron Age oral tradition of the Ganges Valley. The Pāli version of this oral tradition was probably written down in Sri Lanka the first century BCE, while another version was written down in Gāndhārī in the

Peshawar Valley (parts of which were translated into medieval Chinese in the 5th Century); Buddhaghosa and Buddhadatta composed their commentaries in about the 5th century CE in Sri Lanka, supposedly based on existing Sinhala commentaries; and the sub-commentators lived in South India or Sri Lankan in the 13th or 14th century CE. This is a span of almost 2000 years. Behind the relatively conservative Pāli language, the culture is changing all the time. Over this period the Pāli idiom changes quite markedly and some words have changed their meaning or sprouted new connotations. Any problems of this kind that I have identified are reflected in footnotes.

Jayarava
Cambridge, UK.
Aug 2021

Abbreviations

AN	Aṅguttara Nikāya
ANA	Aṅguttara Nikāya Aṭṭhakathā
As	Atthasālinī
Abhi-av	Abhidhammāvatāra
Abhi-av-pṭ	Abhidhammāvatāra-purāṇatīkā
ATI	Access to Insight. http://www.accesstoinsight.org
BHSD	Buddhist Hybrid Sanskrit Dictionary
CST	Chaṭṭha Saṅgāyana Tipiṭaka, Desktop Application, 4th ed.
DN	Dīgha Nikāya
DNA	Sumaṅgalavilāsinī, Dīgha Nikāya Aṭṭhakathā
Dhp	Dhammapada
Dhs-m	Dhammasaṅgaṇi-mātikā (including internal commentary).
DOPN	Dictionary of Pali Names, Online version of the *Dictionary of Pali Proper Names*.
DP	Dictionary of Pāli; Margaret Cone, Pali Text Society.
Mhbh	Mahābhārata.
Mil	Milindapañha
MW	Monier-Williams Sanskrit-English Dictionary
PED	Pali English Dictionary, Pali Text Society.
SA	Saṃyukta Āgama
SN	Saṃyutta Nikāya
SNA	Saṃyutta Nikāya Aṭṭhakathā
Sn	Suttanipāta
Vism	Visuddhimagga

Introduction

Niyāma has become an important concept in the Triratna Buddhist Order, especially since Subhūti's (2010) revision of Sangharakshita's expositions from the 1960s. Sangharakshita and Subhūti presented *niyāma* in terms of "orders of conditionality" that govern reality at different levels. This was, they assured us, a traditional Buddhist teaching, not from the suttas and thus not Buddhavācana,[1] but from Buddhaghosa, one of the founding fathers of the Theravāda sect. Buddhaghosa's various commentaries and manuals formed the basis of Theravāda monastic teachings for centuries. Despite his urging us to adopt a stance of "metaphysical reticence", Subhūti's new scheme made the concept of *niyāma* central to a grand metaphysical scheme describing a cosmic order that subsumed all other forms of human knowledge including all of science. It seemed to me, therefore, all the more important to make the content of these texts available to the Order and the wider Buddhist world.

The modern history of scholarship on the concept of *niyāma* in Buddhism begins in 2009. In an essay for the Order's private journal *Shabda*, Dhīvan began pointing out the texts being referred to as giving the modern doctrine of the so-called "five niyamas" their seal of authenticity were, in fact, quite at odds with Sangharakshita's presentation. Dhīvan traced the origins of the modern interpretation of the "five niyamas" as related to a cosmic order to a work by Caroline Rhys Davids (1912). One of the most interesting, and perhaps underrated characters in the history of European Pāli studies, Rhys Davids creatively reinterpreted the concept of *niyāma* from "constraint" or "fixed course" to "order of causality", and wrote about the five kinds of *niyāma* as forming a hierarchy. As my essay on this hierarchy later in the book shows, this conception shares many features with Auguste Comte's hierarchy of sciences proposed in the mid-nineteenth century.

[1] That is, words supposedly from the mouth of the Buddha.

Rhys Davids was interested in the idea of the universe having a moral order, something missing from Comte's hierarchy. Her presentation of *niyāma* was a way of achieving this without invoking a deity. In Subhūti's account, Rhys Davids' moral order is subsumed into Triratna's metaphysics of *niyāma.*

I begin with a philological investigation of the word, examining the etymology and usage to explain what *niyāma* means and why it means that. Since contemporary use depends on the early modern authors I outline how they contributed to the understanding. These things are dealt with in more detail in Dhīvan Thomas Jones essays for the Order and published articles.[2]

The main part of the book consists of heavily annotated, fairly literal English translations of the texts in question. No doubt, these translations could be improved on but the meaning of the sources texts is conveyed accurately enough for readers to glimpse the intent of the authors and see that they did not have orders of conditionality in mind. They were more concerned to describe constraints on conditionality in relation to sectarian Theravāda Abhidhamma doctrines.

Some partial translations of *sutta* texts that use the word *niyāma* follow. This is mainly for ease of reference since these texts have all been published multiple times. In the case of the *Paccaya Sutta,* I also include a translated passage from the traditional Pāli commentary on the relevant passage, and some notes from my examination of the Chinese counterpart (a translation of a Gāndhārī version of the text).

Finally, I include four essays. The first two essays touch on how the concept of *niyāma* was used in some Sanskrit texts I encountered while reading Sanskrit texts at Cambridge University. The third is my attempt to show the influence on the British Emergentists on Caroline Rhys Davids in her interpretation of *niyāma*, which I think falls short but still sheds some light on the intellectual context in which this neglected, but highly influential figure worked. The last essay is an attempt to explain the differences between different versions of the *Paccaya Sutta* (SN 12:20), which gives us some insights into how Buddhist

---

[2] Dhīvan 2009, 2013; Jones 2012, 2013.

terminology evolves and how Buddhists dealt with this in relation to having a canon of texts.

Thus, in this one small volume, all of the references to *niyāma* in the whole Pāli literature are translated and contextualised and are ready for use in discussions about how we employ the concept of *niyāma* and/or how we understand the universe to be ordered. Combined with Dhīvan's published works, this should enable informed discussion of *niyāma* in English and also leaves a trail of breadcrumbs for those who would take up the study of *niyāma* in Pāli (or Chinese) in the future.

A Word on References to Pāli Suttas.

When citing a Pāli text I will give the name in Pāli followed by the initials of the *Nikāya*, i.e. DN, MN, SN, or AN (see the list of abbreviations). For DN and MN this is followed by the running number of the sutta in the *Nikāya*. For the much longer AN and SN, I give the chapter and running number. For example, the *Paccaya Sutta* (SN 12.20) can be found in the *Saṃyutta Nikāya* chapter 12 (the *Nidāna Saṃyutta*), *sutta* no.20. However, when citing a particular passage I follow scholarly convention and give the volume (in Roman numerals) and page number in the Pali Text Society edition where it is available. Where readers are consulting translations from Pāli, I recommend they use the translations by Bhikkhu Bodhi published by Wisdom Publications. Other reliable translations can be found on the website *Sutta Central.*[3]

For other works with numbered verses, I give the verse number for a general reference or if more specificity is needed volume and page number. Some of the texts are only available as part of the *Chaṭṭha Saṅgāyana Tipiṭaka* (CST) or *6th Council Edition* produced in Burma in the 1960s, and in this case, I give the volume and page number in that edition.

The Pāli commentaries tend to have two names. For example, the commentary (*aṭṭhakathā*) on the *Dīghanikāya* is generically called the

[3] https://suttacentral.net/

Dīghanikāya Aṭṭhakathā but also has the specific title, *Sumaṅgalavilāsinī*. The standard abbreviation for the *Sumaṅgalavilāsinī* is DA or DNA. I tend to use DNA since DA can be confused with the *Dīrgha Āgama*, the Sanskrit title of a parallel collection of lengthy sūtras that is preserved in Chinese. Incidentally, *Aṭṭhakathā* means something like "discussion of the meaning".

The Concept of Niyama

The concept of *niyāma* is not peculiar to Buddhism but can be found in many other Indian religious texts. For example, in Yoga philosophy *niyama* is used in the sense of an ethical precept, i.e. something that restrains behaviour. There is some confusion over the spelling since *niyama* and *niyāma* appear to be used interchangeably. This is further complicated by modern publications that do not employ diacritics, using *niyama* when they mean *niyāma*.

Margaret Cone, a leading Pāli lexicographer, gives each a separate entry in her *Dictionary of Pāli*:

> ***niyama***. "Constraint; restraint; a practice or vow of self-discipline; restriction, limitation; compulsion; a fixed rule, necessity; an invariable practice or experience." (DOP II 598a)

> ***niyāma***. "A fixed rule; a peculiar or specified way or manner; an invariable practice or experience; a determined or inevitable outcome, certainty; an assured state; what leads to an inevitable outcome, the way to an end." (DOP II 599a)

These two forms have considerable crossover and in effect, they mean very similar things. We can distinguish between the two forms morphologically. Both are derived from the verbal root √*yam* "hold". This root appears to have evolved from a Proto-Indo-European root

**iem*, which has two meanings: "hold" and "double". Some related English words include, "even", "Gemini", and "geminate".[4]

With the suffix *ni-*, the verb becomes *niyameti* or *niyacchati* and takes on the meaning of "holding down" or "holding back".[5] The indicative mode of the verb *niyameti* means, "to tie down, hold back." In Sanskrit grammatical analysis (*vyākaraṇa*), *niyama* is used to describe the restrictions that grammar rules place on language use (Aussant 2015).

The other spelling, *niyāma*, derives from the causative form of the verb, *niyāmeti*.[6] The causative indicates the process that causes the action of the verb. Thus, *niyāmeti* means, "to restrain, control, govern, guide". In appendix to the Pali Text Society translation of the *Kathāvatthu*, a para-canonical text, included in the *Abhidhamma Piṭaka*, Caroline Rhys Davids explains that in Pali *niyama* meaning 'fixity' while *niyāma* means 'that which fixes' (Shwe and Rhys Davids 1915: 383). This tells us that, despite the use she put the word to, Rhys Davids also understood *niyama* to derive from the indicative and *niyāma* from the causative.

This distinction between indicative and causative verbs can be subtle and is often lost in Sanskrit and Pāli, especially the latter. Thus, we find that even in Classical Sanskrit, whose lexicon became fixed around the 4th Century BCE, the two words *niyama/niyāma* are already beginning to merge. In the *Aṣṭādhyāyī*,[7] an influential grammar text probably composed in Northwest India around the fourth century, Pāṇini

---

[4] *Indo-European Lexicon* https://lrc.la.utexas.edu/lex/master/0779

[5] Forms like √*yam* → *yacchati* and √*gam* → *gacchati* are common in Sanskrit. The explanation is uncertain but involves conjugations that were assimilated to the present indicative. Pre-historically *yam* would have been *yṃ* with a vocalic (i.e. vowel-like) *ṃ*.

[6] PED erroneously lists *niyāmeti* as a denominative verb, i.e. a noun that has been turned into a verb (as when we speak of Olympic athletes who win medals as "medalling"). However, DOP correctly understands *niyāmeti* as the causative of *niyameti* or *niyacchati*.

[7] *Aṣṭādhyāyī*, is the earliest known example of a comprehensive descriptive grammar in the world. It is still in use today, and when Europeans discovered Sanskrit in the eighteenth entury it helped to spark the development of the modern science of linguistics.

lists *niyama* and *niyāma* as alternative forms of the same word (Katre 1987: 289).

Despite the similarities and confusion, the concept we are dealing with in this book is *niyāma*. To understand how *niyāma* is used in the Pāli commentaries we need to focus on the Buddhist context and we find here that *niyāma* is used in two main ways.

1. Firstly, the Buddha uses *niyāma* to describe the inevitability of conditionality. For example, in the *Paccaya Sutta* (SN 12.20):

> "Whether anyone is awakened or not, these things are true:
> the fact of mental events, the constraints on mental events,
> and specific conditionality."[8]

The point here is that Buddhists believe that rather than a speculative or theoretical point of view, the Buddha observed the actual constraints that apply to mental phenomena (*dhammā*) qua objects of the *manas* or mind sense. Here, they are expressed in three abstract nouns: *dhammaṭṭhitā*, *dhammaniyāmatā*, and *idappaccayatā.* These are respectively the fact that there *are* mental phenomena; the fact that the conditions are required for the result to occur; and that fact that what arises is determined by the type of conditions present. Here *niyāmatā* refers in a general and abstract way to the constraints on mental phenomena. See also my essay on *dhammaniyāmata and idappaccayatā* later in the book.

The Buddha also uses *niyāma* in the *Uppādā Sutta* (AN 3.137) to describe the intrinsic nature of things as impermanent, painful, and non-self:

> "Whether anyone is awakened or not, these things are true:
> the fact of mental events, the constraints on mental events.

---

[8] *uppādā vā tathāgatānaṃ anuppādā vā tathāgatānaṃ, ṭhitāva sā dhātu dhammaṭṭhitatā dhammaniyāmatā idappaccayatā*. (SN II.25)

> All constructs are impermanent... All constructs are disappointing... All mental events are insubstantial.[9]

Again, the implication here is that mental states, being conditioned, are constrained in these ways: being conditioned they are impermanent, such that the presence of the conditions is required and when they cease, the mental state ceases. Being impermanent, mental states are unsatisfactory; all our expectations for everlasting happiness through experiencing pleasure and avoiding pain are disappointed. And finally, the mental events themselves are not substantial. It is a fact (*ṭhita*) that we have experiences, but experiences don't have location, extension in space, or mass, or any of the other qualities of objects.

Walsh translates *dhammatā* as "it is a rule"; or 'it is lawful'. The word *dhammatā* is an abstract noun from *dhamma*; so a first parsing suggests it means something like *dhamma*-ness. However, we have to ask, "Which meaning of *dhamma* is being referred to?" Translators and commentators agree that it is *dhamma* as "nature" (i.e. having a particular nature) as when the Buddha says: *vayadhamma saṅkhārā* "all constructs are perishable"; i.e. they are of a nature (*dhamma*) to decay and die (*vaya*). The text is saying that it is in the nature of things, the nature of the *universe*, that the life events of the Buddha happen as they do. I have no wish to get into the theological debate that necessarily ensues from this statement. I merely wish to establish *what* the text says and *why* it says that. If something has an abstratct nature (*dhamma-tā*), then that nature (*dhamma*) is natural (*dhammatā*) to it. Hence we may translate *ayamettha dhammatā* as "this here is natural" or "in this case it is natural". Alternatively, it is possible to read *dhammatā* in this context as "customary".

2. Secondly, the Buddha refers to the necessity of a good rebirth for an ideal Buddhist. In the *Cakkhu Sutta* (SN 25:1):

---

[9] *uppādā vā, bhikkhave, tathāgatānaṃ anuppādā vā tathāgatānaṃ, ṭhitāva sā dhātu dhammaṭṭhitatā dhammaniyāmatā. sabbe saṅkhārā aniccā ... sabbe saṅkhārā dukkhā ... sabbe dhammā anattā.* (AN I.286)

> Monks, the one who believes in these teachings (*dhammā*) and settles on them is called "one who follows their belief" (*saddhānusārin*), and enters the inevitability of perfection (*sammatta-niyāma*), enters the level of a superior person (*sappurisa*), having surpassed the level of ordinary people (*puthujjana*).[10]

The *saddhānusārin* "faith follower" and *dhammānusārin* "doctrine follower" are two of the seven types of ideal Buddhist. The word for "ideal person" is *ariya-puggala* (literally "noble-man") and here *sappurisa* "true person" is a synonym. Such a person cannot be reborn in a lower realm and having attained the path to awakening, must at least attain the fruit of stream-entry. In this context, *niyāma* once again means "necessity" or "assurance" in relation to the good destiny of one who has faith in the Buddha.[11] This sense is also found in the *Āvaraṇa Sutta* (AN 6.86) translated below. This use of *niyāma* ties it to the word *sammatta* "perfection", which Buddhaghosa links to the limbs (*aṅga*) of the eightfold path (*aṭṭhaṅgika-magga*). He lists eight *sammattas* to correspond with the eight limbs. This sense of *niyāma* is often translated as "fixed course" (c.f. Bodhi 2000: 1004. Translation of SN 25.1); which is just another way of saying 'certain outcome'. In the *Suttanipāta* (Sn 55), *niyāma* appears to be similarly a reference to the assurance of liberation. We find that the use of *niyāma* in practice follows what we would expect from the semantics, which is not always the case with a Buddhist technical term (see for example Attwood 2018a).

Niyama, then, means "restraint, constraint, restriction; inevitability, assurance, necessity" and *niyāma* means "on a fixed or inevitable course", although the forms are thoroughly confused in Pāli and it's no longer always possible to distinguish which was intended. Over the years I have tried out several translations but have come to the

---

[10] *Yo, bhikkhave, ime dhamme evaṃ saddahati adhimuccati – ayaṃ vuccati saddhānusārī, okkanto sammattaniyāmaṃ, sappurisabhūmiṃ okkanto, vītivatto puthujjanabhūmiṃ* (SN III.225)

[11] *Saddhā* is the cognate of Latin credo "I believe". Contrary to popular belief, in Pāli *saddhā* expresses faith *in the Buddha*. It is not the confidence born of effective practice, which is referred to as *avecca-passada*.

conclusion that "fixed course" best fits Buddhaghosa use of the term. Still, a reader must keep in mind the other possibilities for shades of meaning. Now we need to consider the specific use of the concept of *niyāma* in the formulation: *pañcavidha-niyāma* or "five-fold constraint"

The Five-fold Niyāma

The Pāli texts do not speak of "five niyamas" (*pañcā niyāmā*), but of a single *niyāma* that is of five kinds (*pañcavidho niyāmo*). The word *vidha* means "of a kind, consisting of, -fold", so *pañcavidho niyāmo* means "fivefold constraint" or "a constraint consisting of five kinds". The five kinds of *niyāma* are *bīja-niyāma*, *utu-niyāma*, *kamma-niyāma*, *citta-niyāma*, and *dhamma-niyāma*, i.e. seed-constraint, season-constraint, action-constraint, thought-constraint, and nature-constraint (or religious-constraint). The order in which the five are given is variable in the texts.

Bīja is the standard word for "seed" in both Pāli and Sanskrit. It is used both literally to refer to actual seeds and figuratively to refer to anything that is the indirect or distal cause of an event. The maturation process of a seed becoming a mature plant with fruit is a popular source of analogies in Indian philosophy.

Utu refers to the change of seasons. The Sanskrit equivalent *ṛtu* has more or less the same range of meanings as Pāli *utu* (c.f. MW). It may be that we can connect *ṛtu* with *ṛta* "the cosmic order" since they both derive from PIE **ar* "to fit together". Note that Pāli lacks this word, but the form would be **uta*. English has many words from this root including: "arm" and "art" and all their derivative and associated forms, e.g. "order", "rate", "ratio". Sayadaw (1978) renders *utu-niyāma* as "caloric order". In this, he is most likely following the medieval Abhidhamma textbook *Abhidhammattha Saṅgaha* (Bodhi 1993) in which *utu* comes to mean "temperature", and refers to the influence of the fire element in the origination of material phenomena (1993: 250). The date of this text is not well established but it was probably composed the 12th century). This late interpretation does not apply to the 5th century texts which form the basis of the interpretation of *utuniyāma*. The meaning of the word *utu* (and thus *utu-nyāma*) in the

Sumaṅgalavilāsinī, *Atthasālinī*, and *Abhidhammāvatāra* (and its commentaries) is cyclic seasonal phenomena, for example, the flowering and fruiting of trees in the same season throughout the land; winds; the heat of the sun in different seasons; and the day-night cycles.

The role of the fivefold niyāma in the commentaries seems to be to naturalise Buddhist ideas about three unseen or supernatural processes: mental processes (*citta*); the functioning of *karma*; and the miracles associated with a Buddha.[12] This is done by likening them to observable processes in nature. So we have *bīja-niyāma* or "the fixed course of seeds" that describes rice seeds becoming rice plants and producing rice grains; and *utu-niyāma*, the fact that trees flower and fruit together in the appropriate season. These are limitations or restrictions (*niyama*) on how natural events unfold that result in a fixed course of events (*niyāma*) that can be observed by everyone in nature. And these then form a common model of understanding other kinds of processes, especially ones with a less obvious mechanism, such as karma or thoughts.

The Buddhist model of cognition is a result, to some extent, of introspection by yogis. We can only ever observe our own cognitive processes and never someone else's (at least this limitation applies in Iron Age India). However, Buddhists felt confident in providing a generalised description of cognition all the same. The Theravādin *Abhidharma* model is called *cittavīthi* and features in the explanations of *cittaniyāma*. Similarly, the process of *karma*—the idea that good and evil deeds have appropriate consequences for the appropriate person at the appropriate time—is unseen and supernatural. *Karma* operates behind the scenes. It is an article of faith. The various miracles mentioned in the life history of a Buddha are also supernatural and by the time the *niyāma* doctrine is composed, the historical Buddha had been dead for many centuries.

---

[12] I should emphasise that I do not mean "naturalise" in the modern sense of the word, but only according to what was considered natural *at the time*, in particular examples drawn from nature and especially from agriculture. Many ontological dualists claim that the mind is somehow supernatural – made of a distinct "stuff" from the natural world and not bound by the laws of the physical world.

Analogical thinking is particularly important in Indian thought. The argument about *niyāma* set out in the commentaries is that the limitations on the *visible* processes of seeds and seasons are analogous to the *invisible* processes of karma and mental activity. The analogy of *karma* with the process of planting seeds and reaping grain was one that appealed to the Indian mind because a more literal version of this same analogy became the main Mahāyāna view of *karma*. The "seeds" were even provided with a metaphorical storage container in the form of the *ālayavijñāna*.

In the *Sumaṅgalavilāsinī* and the *Atthasālinīi*, Buddhaghosa is concerned to establish the invisible processes of cognition, *karma*, and miracles as *natural* in the same way as visible processes of seeds growing into fruits in the right season. Buddhaghosa is particularly focussed on *karma* as a natural process characterised by inevitability, by results that are appropriate to the cause, and by ripening in due season. The later commentators shifted their focus from *karma* to *citta* in line with the pre-eminence of the *Abhidhamma* in Theravāda Buddhism. Buddhaghosa uses the same argument to establish that the miracles associated with the life events of a Buddha are also natural.

For some modern commentators, the point of niyāma was to insist that not all events are the result of *karma*. However, early Buddhists acknowledge from the outset that *karma* is not the only cause of experience as is clear from the *Sīvaka Sutta* (SN 36.21).

> Venerable Gotama, there are some religieux who have a doctrine or view: "whatever pain or pleasure a person experiences is all due to former actions. What does the venerable Gotama say about this?
>
> Some feelings arise from bile (*pitta*), this one can know for oneself, and is considered true in the world. Therefore, what those religieux say is false.
>
> Some feelings arise from phlegm (*semha*) ...from wind (*vāta*); from unions of humours (*sannipātika*)... from seasons (*utu*)... from attacks, adversity, and deprivation

> (*visamaparihārajāni*)[13]... from spasms (*opakkamika*)... and from the fruition of kamma.... Therefore, what those religieux say is false.

Contrarily, judging by the commentarial accounts, Theravādins were coming around to the idea that even these other conditions for suffering are ultimately caused by karma (see Bodhi's notes 2000: 1436 n.253).

The concept of *niyāma* was popularised in the late 20th Century by Sangharakshita as "the five niyamas"[14] presumably based on earlier formulations by Caroline Rhys Davids and Ledi Sayadaw.[15] Caroline Rhys Davids summarises this view:

> "This order which Buddhism saw in the universe was called in Pali *niyāma*, that is, 'going-on, process'. In its five branches, strands, phases were discerned: *kamma-niyama*, order of act-and-result; *utu-niyama*, physical (inorganic) order; *bīja-niyama*, order of germs, or seeds (physical organic order); chitta-niyama, order of mind, or conscious life; dhamma-niyāma, order of the norm, or the effort of nature to produce a perfect type." (1912: 119)

The ordering of the *niyāmas* used by Rhys Davids and Sangharakshita does not occur in any source text.

---

[13] Bodhi translates according to the commentary: "careless behaviour". I take the compound *visama-parihāra-jāni* as a *dvandva*, i.e. as three related but distinct causes. For more on the terms *pitta*, *semha*, and *vāta* in Indian though see Scharfe 1999.

[14] "Niyama" here has effectively been anglicized so it loses its diacritics and italics.

[15] We say "presumably" because Sangharakshita does not reference his sources in this case. However, his formulation is so similar to Rhys Davids' and he was known to be an enthusiast of her work that this seems to be the natural conclusion. Subhūti uncritically cites Ledi Sayadaw's translation of the *Athasālini*.

Compounds

A final linguistic issue is that the words used for the five different kinds of *niyāma* are compounds: *bīja-niyāma*, *utu-niyāma*, *kamma-niyāma*, *citta-niyāma*, and *dhamma-niyāma*. These compounds can be read two different ways which lend themselves to different translations. If we use the example of *dhamma-niyāma* then we can read it as a genitive *tatpuruṣa* compound "the inevitability of nature" or as a *karmadhāraya* "the nature constraint".

My inclination is to treat the compounds as types of *niyāma* and thus to read them as *karmadhāraya*. However, one of the historical experts on Sanskrit grammar, Patañjali, gives a *vyākaraṇa* or grammatical analysis of the (Sanskrit) compound *dharma-niyama* in his *Vyākaraṇa-Mahābhāṣya*, a commentary on Sanskrit grammar probably from the 2nd Century BCE. Patañjali says:

> What is dharma-niyama? It is a restriction for religion (*dharmāya niyamaḥ*); or, a restriction for the purpose of religion (*dharmārthaḥ vā niyamaḥ*); or a restriction aiming at religion (*dharmaprayojanaḥ vā niyamaḥ*).[16]

We can see that Patañjali reads *dharma-niyama* as a dative *tatpuruṣa* compound. Being part of the Vedic milieu he also reads *dharma* in terms of the duties incumbent on religieux. It's possible that *dharma-niyama* read in isolation is intended as a *tatpuruṣa*, but that when Buddhaghosa coined the other four terms and referred to the different types as pañcavidha, he appears to have been thinking more in terms of *karmadhāraya*. On the other hand, one should keep in mind that *bīja-niyāma* can be read as "seed-constraint" and "the fixed course of seed [maturation]".

Having surveyed the meanings and uses of the word *niyāma*, we can now turn to the sources themselves.

---

[16] For the full passage and citation see my essay "Dharma-niyama in the *Vyākaraṇa-Mahābhāṣya*" later in the book.

Fivefold Niyāma Translations

I made use of the CST electronic version of the Pāli Tripiṭaka to identify all the texts that make use of the concept of the *pañcavidha-niyāma*, or fivefold-*niyāma*. A total of five texts were identified and then translated. These are:

Sumaṅgalavilāsinī (DNA 2.431). The commentary on the *Dīghanikāya*, composed by Buddhaghosa ca. 5th century in Sri Lanka. Specifically the section on the *Mahāpadāna Sutta* (DN 14).

Atthasālinī (As 272-274). A commentary on the *Dhammasaṅgaṇi* (an *Abhidhamma* text)[17] composed by Buddhaghosa ca. 5th century in Sri Lanka.

Abhidhammāvatāra (CST Abhi-av 66; vs. 468-473; PTS 54). A verse summary of *Abhidhamma* attributed to Buddhadatta, composed in South Indian, ca. 5th Century CE.

Abhidhamma-mātikā (CST Dhs-m 58). An internal commentary on the *mātika* or matrix associated with the *Dhammasaṅgaṇī* composed in South India by Coḷaraṭṭha Kassapa (12–13th C).

Abhidhammāvatāra-purāṇatīkā (Abhi-av-pṭ 1.68). A sub-commentary on the *Abhidhammāvatāra Nāmarūpa-parichedo*, composed in Sri Lanka by Vācissara Mahāsāmi ca. 13th century or by Sāriputta ca. 12th century.

With the longer texts, I have I translated only that portion of the text that deals with *niyāma*. In addition, the word *niyāma* is used in other contexts within the suttas. Since many of the discussions about the word *niyāma* refer back to these texts, I thought it would be advantageous to

[17] Previously translated in Rahula (1974) although I have not seen this article.

include translations of the relevant passages in this book (making it a one-stop-shop). The words used and the texts that represent how they were used are as follows.

- *dhamma-niyāmatā*: *Paccaya Sutta* (SN 12.20); *Uppādā Sutta* (A 3.134)
- *niyāma*:[18] *Āvaraṇa Sutta* (AN 6.86)
- *sammatta-niyāma*: *Cakkhu Sutta* (SN 25.1)

A note on conventions in these translations.

Ideally, a translator will create a new text that alleviates the need to refer to the text being translated. However, the translation process seldom reaches that ideal. In practice, translation is a compromise. In religious texts that make liberal use of technical jargon, it is important to make it clear which technical terms are being used to enable readers to make comparisons, check definitions in dictionaries, and so on. At best, a translation will imply the underlying term. Second best, is to establish a convention by which the reader will see the word and understand that despite any connotations in the target language, it has a definite meaning in the source language. When all else fails, or the translator's art fails them, the technical term has to be given either in a note or in parentheses in the text. In a first translation, the translator is obligated to minimise ambiguity, so here I have frequently resorted to the crudest method. Perhaps if these texts ever become popular enough to warrant a subsequent translation, a more sophisticated approach may be taken. One final strategy is to leave a word untranslated and explain it outside the text in notes. This is not translation per se but sometimes its seems simpler to give the word in Pāli an explain it rather than choose a misleading English word and try to explain that (because we also have to explain what it does not mean).

[18] The word occurs rarely in the *Nikāyas* and mostly in the *Aṅguttara Nikaya*: AN 3.22, 5.151, 5.152, 5.153, 6.86, 6.87, 6.88; also Sn v.55. All of the AN texts combine *niyāma* with forms of *okkamati* and *sammatta* and so are in fact related to SN 25.1 (*okkanto sammatta-niyāma*)

The translator can seldom find a word for word translation of a source text in the target language. Languages are not amenable to this kind of treatment. Usually, it is better to think of the sentence as the smallest unit of meaning that is translated. In the case of Buddhist translations, we often see the practice of retaining the syntax of the source language to "preserve the original". This practice is common enough to have been bestowed the polemical sobriquet *Buddhist Hybrid English.* In general, resorting to Buddhist Hybrid English is poor practice and is now widely disparaged amongst translators.

In trying to produce good English, or when the original author assumes a great deal in their text, or when the original author abbreviates something in a way that will be confusing to a modern reader, the translator has to *add* something to the text. These additions, interpolations, or explanations are conventionally placed within square brackets, though again notes may be used. The principle is that the translator makes clear that these additions are not in the text per se, but are implied or required in order to make comprehensible English. The result is a text peppered with parenthetical clutter that can be off-putting and breaks up the flow of the text. It certainly does not add to the readability of the text. However, in a first translation, the additional information conveyed makes it worth it for the reader and the student of the history of ideas. These are not texts to be read for pleasure or recited in a ritual, so we can justify sacrificing readability for maximising the information conveyed. The primary goal here is to make the ideas in the source texts available to a modern reader and this often requires the translator to provide the necessary context.

Notes are for extraneous information that the translator has discovered or thinks it would be useful for the reader to have at hand. Whereas many books place this information at the end of the book, where it is out of the way, but also less accessible, I opt for footnotes so that any additional information accompanies the text it comments on. This is particularly important for a previously untranslated text since there may be much that is unfamiliar to the reader. In the case of the intended audience for these translations, I assume that while some will have read suttas in translation, very few readers will be familiar with the Pali commentarial traditions of 5th or 13th Century Sri Lanka and South

India and thus I have been liberal with notes. I have included anything and everything that I have discovered along the way that helped to illuminate the text for me, in the hope that others will find it illuminating. The aim is to create a reference work on the concept of *niyāma*, which may in time give rise to more accessible discussions.

I debated including the Pāli text along side the translation. But I don't think this helps the reader who doesn't know Pāli and the reader who does can easily get access to the text if they wish to.

Sumaṅgalavilāsinī

(DNA 2.431)

The *Sumaṅgalavilāsinī* (*Dīghanikāya-aṭṭhakathā*) is Buddhaghosa's commentary on the *Dīgha Nikāya* composed ca. 5th Century in Sri Lanka.[19]

In this first use of *pañca niyāma*, Buddhaghosa is commenting on a passage from the *Mahāpadāna Sutta* (DN II.12[20]) that deals with the miracles accompanying the keys events in the biography of a Buddha:

> "It is natural, bhikkhus, that having fallen from the company of contented gods,[21] a bodhisatta enters his mother's belly… this is natural".[22]

[Buddhaghosa says]: "this is natural"—here entering the mother's belly is natural (*dhammatā*) and is called "this nature" (*sabhāva*),[23] "this fixed course" (*niyāma*). And the five-fold fixed course has these names: the fixed course of actions (*kamma-niyāma*); the fixed course of seasons (*utu-niyāma*); the fixed course of seeds (*bīja-niyāma*); the fixed course

---

[19] The text was previously translated by Walpola Rahula (1974).

[20] *dhammatā, esā, bhikkhave, yadā bodhisatto tusitā kāyā cavitvā mātukucchiṃ okkamati… Ayamettha dhammatā.*

[21] In my book on karma and rebirth (Attwood 2019) I show that there are two main uses of the word *kāya*: 1. a human body; and 2. a group. Here it refers to the group or company of devas who are satisfied (*tusita*). The word *tusita* being from √*tuṣ* "be content". These devas are thus contrasted with "the departed" (*peta* aka the 'the hungry ghosts') who are not able to be content.

[22] The term *dhammatā* is then used to describe all the miraculous events of the Buddha's hagiography. However *dhammatā* can also mean "customary", which would work equally well here.

[23] The word *sabhāva* later becomes a technical term in Mahāyāna Buddhism in its Sanskrit guise *svabhāva*. Here it just means "state (of mind), nature, condition" (PED).

of mental events (*citta-niyāma*); and the fixed course of nature (*dhamma-niyāma*).[24]

This [principle of] "giving of pleasant consequences for skilfulness, and unpleasant results for unskilfulness", is the "fixed course of actions". There is an illustration. The grounds for this are in the [*Dhammapada*] verse:

> Not in the sky, nor the middle of the ocean,
> Nor in a mountain cave;
> Though terrified there is nowhere on earth,
> Where one might escape from an evil action.[25]

Moreover, once a woman quarrelled with her husband and strangled him. Then wanting to die herself she put a noose around her neck. A certain man was sharpening a knife and saw her about to hang herself. Wanting to cut the rope, he ran up to relieve her [calling] 'don't be afraid, don't be afraid.' The rope turned into a snake and he froze. Frightened, he ran. Shortly afterwards the woman died. Thus the danger should be obvious.[26]

The trees in all the provinces acquire fruit and flowers etc. all at the same time[27]; the wind blowing or not blowing; the quickness or slowness of the sun's heat; the devas sending rain or not; day blossoming lotuses withering at night; this and similar things are the inevitability of seasons.

---

[24] Note the order of the aspects of *niyāma* here: *kamma, utu, bīja, citta, dhamma*. This certainly does not fit modern hierarchical accounts.

[25] This is *Dhammapada* 127. Note the verse illustrates the principle of inevitablity rather than the principle of the appropriateness of results. The inevitability of karma was a given for Buddhaghosa, but this was eroded in other sects as time went on (see Attwood 2014).

[26] What is obvious to the author is far from obvious to me. As best as I can make out this is a magical allegorical story—the rope turns into a snake to prevent the man from saving the woman, because this would have meant that she escaped from the fate she deserves after having strangled her husband.

[27] Pāli: *ekappahāreneva* literally 'with just one blow.

From the rice seed comes only rice fruit; from a sweet fruit comes only sweet flavour, and from a bitter fruit comes only bitter taste. This is the fixed course of seeds.[28]

From the first aspects of mind and mental events (*citta-cetasikā dhammā*) to the last, each is conditioned by a condition or precondition (*upanissaya-paccayena*). Thus that which comes forth from eye-cognition etc.[29] is immediately in agreement [with that cognition].[30] [This is the fixed course of mental events]

The shaking of the 10,000 world system when the bodhisatta enters his mother's belly and other such phenomena [associated with the life story of the Buddha as told in the *Mahāpadāna Sutta*], this is called the nature constraint (*dhamma-niyāma*). The fixed course of nature is understood as consisting in this. This meaning is indicated in the text that begins "this, bhikkhus, is *dhammatā*."

---

[28] Note that "sweet" and "bitter" here are probably allusions to *kusala* and *akusala*.

[29] Meaning ear, nose, tongue, body and mind cognition.

[30] The point here seems to be the one made in the *Mahātaṅhasaṅkhaya Sutta* (M 38) from whatever condition cognition arises, it is named after that. The cognition that arises on condition of eye and form is eye-cognition: (*yaññadeva, bhikkhave, paccayaṃ paṭicca uppajjati viññāṇaṃ thena teneva saṅkhaṃ gacchati. cakkuñca paṭicca rūpe uppajjati viññāṇaṃ, cakkhuviññāṇan-t-eva saṅkhaṃ gacchati* - M i.259). So a contact between eye and form does not give rise to ear cognition (the formula takes no account of synaesthesia). In a sense the point here is the same as the inevitability of seeds: you can't have ear cognition from eye contact.

Atthasālinī

As 272-274

The *Atthasālinī* is Buddhaghosa's commentary on the *Dhammasaṅgaṇi* (aka *Dhammasaṅgani-Aṭṭhakathā*), a text from the *Abhidhamma Piṭaka*; it was composed ca. 5th Century, Sri Lanka.[31]

In this place what's called the "five-fold fixed course" is comprehended, i.e. the fixed course of seeds, the fixed course of seasons, the fixed course of actions, the fixed course of nature, and the fixed course of mental events.

In this case, grass and shrubs grow upwards; a right-handed creeper grows around the tree to the right; Sunflowers turn to face the sun; a vine grows by turning towards the tree; a coconut tree with its head cut off doesn't grow; the seed always gives a similar fruit—this is the fixed course of seeds.[32]

The fact that trees acquire flowers, fruits, and sprouts all in one go is called the fixed course of seasons.[33]

Actions connected with three causes give results connected with three or two causes or no cause. Actions connected with two causes give results connected with two causes or no cause and do not give results connected with three causes.[34] Getting a result that is similar to the cause

[31] This text was previously translated by Ledi Sayadaw (1965).

[32] Note that here *bīja-niyāma* is used in a slightly broader sense than in the *Sumaṅgalavilāsinī.*

[33] Note that in Ledi Sayadaw's translation, the word *utu* has changed its meaning from when Buddhaghosa composed this text. Sayadaw follows the later Theravāda *Abhidhamma* in thinking of it as "heat", but this is clearly *not* what was intended here.

[34] The number of causes—*tihetu*, *duhetu* (or *dvihetu*) and *ahetu*—are terms only found in the commentaries to the *Abhidhamma*, particularly in the *Atthasālinī* and the *Abhidhammāvatāra*. Each refers to a type of rebirth (*paṭisandhi*). The three *hetu* are the opposites of the three poisons: craving, hatred, and confusion (*lobha*, *dosa*, & *moha*), i.e. contentment (*alobha*), kindness (*adosa*), and understanding (*amoha*). A being that possesses three causes (*tihetu* i.e.

is called the fixed course of actions. Additionally, it is called "the fixed course of actions" because the result is in accordance with the action.[35]

There are stories that illustrate this. Such as the crow that was flying along when a blade of grass rose up from a fire, and caught the crow around the neck and killed him. [36] Also, the sailors who were becalmed on the great ocean. They passed around straws to see who should be expelled from the ship. [At this point the commentary tells us that the lot fell three times to the wife of the captain]. There's only one action to prevent us from all perishing: we must throw her overboard! The captain said, "I can't bear to see her floating in the water", so tie a pot of sand to her neck and throw her overboard. Then a bold man seized the opportunity and threw her overboard. One bhikkhu entered a cave and the mountain top fell down blocking the entrance. On the seventh day he was freed [when the boulder blocking the entrance miraculously moved itself].

The perfect Buddha sitting in the Jeta Grove teaching the Dhamma related these three examples at one time. The Teacher, seeing the past [actions] repeated, said: "not that [action] done by another; but the action done by you!"

The crow was a man in a previous life. Unable to master one of his oxen, he wound a braid of straw around its neck and set fire to it, killing the ox. Now given that, he could not escape his action by flying through the air.[37] The woman [on the ship] was also a woman in a previous life.

---

alobha, *adosa*, & *amoha*) can only be reborn in the human realm or a god realm; a being with none (*ahetu*) will be reborn in the lower worlds (*apāya* = animal, *peta* (ghost), *asura* (demon), and hell realms), or if in the human realm afflicted by some disability. The fate of the *duhetu-paṭsandhika* (the one who is reborn with two causes) is not specified. (Nyanaponika 2004, p.167).

[35] This is the same principle as the seed always giving the same kind of fruit: apples from apple seeds, never apples from orange seeds.

[36] This and the subsequent stories come from the commentary on *Dhammapada* verse 127, which is also cited in the *Sumaṅgalavilāsinī*. In each of these stories something bad happens in this life due to an evil action in the past. Each one explains part of the verse. This is a deterministic view of kamma in which a misfortune in this life is caused by having done a similar action in the past. This would appear to be the orthodox Theravāda view of *kamma*.

[37] Note that the manner of his death is determined by the way that he killed the ox in a past-life.

A dog becoming acquainted with her, followed when she went to the wilderness and returned with her. People mocked her saying, "here come the hunter and her dog." Upset by this and unable to restrain the dog, she tied a pot of sand around its neck and threw it in the water. And because of that, she could not escape even in the middle of the ocean. Similarly, the bhikkhu was a cowherd in a previous life, [and seeing] a lizard enter a hole he covered it up with bunches of sticks. However, seven days later he returned and uncovered it. The terrified lizard emerged. Out of compassion, he did not kill it. He too could not escape his action though he sat in a mountain cave. These three reasons being combined were put into this verse [Dhp 127]:

Not in the sky, nor the middle of the ocean,
Nor in a mountain cave;
Though terrified there is nowhere on earth,
Where one might escape from an evil action.

This is called the fixed course of actions. Other types of reasons could also be given.

The shaking of the ten thousand world systems when the bodhisatta takes rebirth, comes out from his mother's belly, attaining of perfect awakening of the Tathāgata, turning of the wheel of the Dhamma, release from the components of life, and the complete extinction—this is called the fixed course of nature.

However in the striking of a sense organ (*pasāda*)[38] by a sense object (*ārammaṇa*)[39]—what you advert to (*āvajjana*), that you become; what you go to (*javana*) you become".[40] There is no doer, nor anyone who causes it to be done. For anyone, however, from the time of striking

---

[38] This sense of *pasāda* "clear, bright; joy, satisfaction" is peculiar to the Abhidhamma.

[39] The primary sense of *ārammaṇa* is "foundation" (c.f. *dhamma*). Early Buddhist theories of perception involve a sense object (*ārammaṇa*) striking a sense faculty (*indriya*) in the presence of sense cognition (*viññāṇa*). The *Abhidhamma* expanded on this considerably.

[40] The reference here is to a detailed *Abhidharma* model of the stages of cognition. See Nyanatiloka (2004) sv. *āvajjana* and *javana*.

of sense organ by sense object, [consciousness of the object] begins with the functional mind-element consciousness (*kiriya-manodhātu-citta*) [41] causing an excitation in the subconscious (*bhavaṅga*[42]), eye-cognition (*cakkhu-viññāṇa*) accomplishes the functions of perception (*dassana-kicca*), the resultant mind-element (*vipāka-mano-dhātu*) accomplishes the function of receiving (*sampaṭicchana-kicca*), the resultant mental cognition element (*vipāka-mano-viññāṇa-dhātu*) accomplishes the function of examining [the object] (*santīraṇa-kicca*), the functional mental cognition element (*kiriya-mano-viññāṇa-dhatu*) accomplishes the function of determining [the nature of the object] (*voṭṭhapana-kicca*), and impulse (*javana*) experiences the nature (*rasa*) of sense-objects (*ārammaṇa*). This is called the fixed course of mental events. This is understood. [43]

---

[41] The function (*kiriyā*) of *manodhātu* in Abhidhamma thinking is to cause advertence (*āvajjana*) towards sense objects; and a *citta* is a moment of consciousness.

[42] *Bhavaṅga* or *bhavaṅga-citta* is a uniquely Theravāda addition to the Buddhist conception of the cognitive process, designed to bridge the gap in moments of unconsciousness and at death. The mental event at death (*cuti-citta*) gives rise to a mental event that forms the link (*paṭisandhi-citta*) between one life and the next. *Bhavaṅga* is the first moment of the new life and has the same object as the *paṭisandhi-citta*. *Bhavaṅga* is present in every moment that a sensory mental event does not arise and each time it is identical. See also Attwood (2018).

[43] This is an outline of part of an *Abhidhamma* analysis of the process of cognition known broadly as *cittavīthi* or "cognitive series", which describes in detail the process by which the mind cognises sensory data. The *cittavīthi* is described (in great detail) at Vism XIV.111 ff. (= Ñāṇamoli 1997: 514 ff.). See also Ronkin (2005: 218) which takes a different approach to translation. Another resource is Nyanatiloka's *Buddhist Dictionary*. Don't panic if you don't understand this long, highly convoluted, and jargon laden sentence. What it boils down to is a highly scholastic *Abhidhammika* version of the processes of cognition. All that is necessary is to understand that the *citta-niyāma* refers to the fixed course of mental events.

Abhidhammāvatāra Nāmarūpa-parichedo

A verse summary of *Abhidhamma* attributed to Buddhadatta, a South Indian contemporary of Buddhaghosa, ca. 5th Century CE.[44]

468. The fixed course of seasons and seeds, actions and nature;
And the fixed course of mental events should be known as the five fixed courses (*pañca niyāmatā*).[45]

469. Regarding the bearing of fruits and flowers all in one blow,
By all the trees; this is the fixed course of seasons.

470. Whatever the seed, it becomes a comparable fruit
The beheaded coconut tree [doesn't grow],[46] this is the result of the seed (*bījajo*)[47]

471. Three causes, two causes and no cause;[48]
Give the appropriate result: this is the fixed course of actions.

472. The birth of a bodhisatta being accompanied by the shaking of the earth,

---

[44] The text is in verse. One line of translation corresponds to one line of verse, but I've made no attempt to put it into metre.

[45] The two terms *niyāma* and its abstract counterpart *niyāmatā* "inevitability" seem to be used synonymously in this verse, probably *metri causa*, i.e. for the sake of the metre.

[46] This is an allusion: "cutting off the head of a coconut tree" (*matthake nāḷikerassa, chiddattaṃ*). If you cut the head of a coconut tree or a palm tree, then unlike other trees it will die. Another agricultural illusion sometimes used alongside this one is that a banana shoot dies when it has fruited. The coconut allusion suggests that *bīja* refers to all the different ways that plants reproduce and grow.

[47] Presumable *bījaniyāma* is abbreviated here to fit the metre, but *bījaja* gives us a further insight into the meaning of *niyāma* since the suffix *–ja* comes from √*jan* "to bring forth, produce, cause".

[48] On the various causes see note 31.

And the many universes etc, this is the fixed course of nature.

473. Hit in the sense-organ by the sense-field, however;[49]
Adverting to the production, this is the fixed course of mental events.[50]

[49] In the Pāli model of sense cognition, the sense object hits the sense organ producing a sensation.

[50] This is a very brief allusion to a more complex model which is given in more detail above in the last part of the *Atthasālinī* passage.

Abhidhammāvatāra-purāṇatīkā

This text was composed by in Sri Lanka by Vācissara Mahāsāmi ca. 13th century or by Sāriputta ca. 12th Century. The *Purāṇātīka* ("ancient sub-commentary") is a commentary on the text of the *Abhidhammāvatāra Nāmarūpa-parichedo* (a *ṭīka* or subcommentary) so is technically a sub-subcommentary. This commentary is an incomplete word by word commentary – words from the text being commented on are in bold (with the Pāli in parentheses or notes).

[468.] **The fixed course of seasons and seeds** (*utubījaniyāma*) means the fixed course of seasons (*utuniyāma*) and the fixed course of seeds (*bījaniyāma*). And **the fixed course of actions and nature** means the fixed course of actions and the fixed course of nature, such as the perfection of ethics etc[51]; and the fixed course of mental events (*cittassa niyāmo*[52]); [and these] five states of constraint (*niyāmatā*) should be known by the learned (*paṇḍita*).

[469.] **There** [means] amongst these five fixed courses, all of the trees fruit & flowers etc all at once bear in season, this is the fixed course of seasons (*ujuniyāmatā*).

[470.] **Whatever the seed, it becomes a comparable fruit**: for a given seed, the fruit of the crop that arises is the same, this is the fixed course of seeds. **The beheaded coconut tree** means the fruit of the coconut tree comes from the head [and cutting off the head means there

---

[51] Pāli *sīlādi-pāramī-dhamma-niyāmatā*. One of the ways that *dhamma* can be translated is "list item" it is regularly used in this sense to the list of items typically called *nidānas* in English. In fact the list items as *dhammas*, and the relationship between them is that each *dhamma* forms the basis (*nidāna*) for the next. The author of this sub-commentary reads *dhammaniyāma* in this way. The reference to the perfections here contradicts Buddhaghosas understanding of *dhamma-niyāma*.

[52] Here the author has resolved the compound *cittaniyāma* as a genitive *tatpuruṣa*, i.e. "fixed course (*niyāma*) of a mental event (*cittassa*)" which is how I have been reading the compounds throughout.

will not be any fruit]; **the state of being cut**[53] (*chiddaataṃ*) [means] being cut (*chiddabhāva*); **this is the result of the seed** (*ayaṃ bījajo*) means the inevitability of being born from a seed (*bījato jāto niyāmo*).[54]

[471.] A three cause action and a three cause result, and a two cause result, and an uncaused result, give the appropriate result, this is the fixed course of actions.[55]

[472.] **The birth of a bodhisatta** means: a nascent conqueror (*jinaṅkura*) born at the appointed moment being accompanied by the shaking of the earth in many ways, this is the fixed course of nature, such as the perfection of ethics etc.[56]

(473.) **While being hit in the sense-organ by this sense field**; **here** (*idha*) means in this process of thought; **adverting to** means the production of thoughts (*cittānaṃ uppatti*). This is the fixed course of mental events.

---

[53] This is difficult to fit with my translation of the text in the *Abhidhammāvatāra Nāmarūpa-parichedo*. The verse has *matthake nāḷikerassa chiddattaṃ...* which means "having cut the head from the coconut tree." And this sentence is split into two bits by the commentary so the previous comment comments on *matthake nāḷikerassa* "from the head of the coconut"; whereas this comment glosses *chiddattaṃ* (an abstract noun from *chidda* "cutting") with *chiddabhāvo* "the state of being cut" which is sensible in isolation, but doesn't seem to help in the context. It also seems to result in the strange punctuation of the verse which separates "cutting" and "the head of the coconut" into two phrases whereas they are more obviously part of the same phrase.

[54] The Pāli *bījajo* and *bījato jāto* are equivalents "born from a seed".

[55] The commentary just paraphrases *Abhidhammāvatāra Nāmarūpa-parichedo*. See notes on the original of verse 471.

[56] The commentary does not really help explain the use of the perfections as an example here.

Abhidhammamātikā

Internal Commentary

The Abhidhammamātikā is a matrix[57] of abstracts for the *Abhidhamma*, with lists of pairs and triplets of terms from which the whole of the text can theoretically be reconstructed. The passage on the *niyāmas* is from an internal commentary on the *mātika* associated with the *Dhammasaṅgaṇī* (the *niyāmas* don't appear to be mentioned in the *mātrix* itself, but only in this appendix.). It was composed in South India by Coḷaraṭṭha Kassapa (12–13th Century.).

The five-fold fixed course: the fixed course of seeds, the fixed course of seasons, the fixed course of actions, the fixed course of nature, and the fixed course of mental events.

Regards this, from the seeds of the different kinds of tree, grass, shrubs, creepers, and celestial trees come the same kind of fruit. This is called the fixed course of seeds.

The way that trees all get their sprouts, flowers and fruits all in one go, at the same time, this called the fixed course of seasons. Actions which are skilful or unskilful give results of the same kind; give results in accordance with the action. This is called the fixed course of actions.

The bodhisatta taking rebirth, emerging from his mother's belly, and the thirty-two portentous signs[58] including the awakening and turning of the wheel of the *Dhamma*. This is called the fixed course of nature.

---

[57] The words *mātika* and *matrix* are cognate and have almost the same meanings.

[58] *Pubbanimitta*, literally "signs from the past", i.e. signs that precede events, or portents. The traditional four sights (old age, sickness, death and the seeker) are also referred to as *pubbanimitta*. The 32 portents are probably the list referred to in *acchariya-abbhūta Sutta* (MN 123) which lists an unnumbered series of miraculous events associated with the birth of the *bodhisatta*.

According to the way it's said that the successive functions of the subconscious (*bhavaṅga*) and impulses (*āvajjana*) etc.[59] manifest in the mind (*cittappavatti*). This is called the fixed course mental events.

[60]{Now however by the fixed course of mental events should be understood—the twenty-five impulses of the cognitive mind element occurring successively amongst mind and mental events [61] having functions, [and] according to their origin, states with a single function,[62] and the remaining states with two, three, four or five functions formerly mentioned.[63] And thus referring to one door etc.[64] And according to the classification on account of functions and [sense] doors of the mind and mental events should be understood. However there is this distinction—function is concerned with everything (14) doing functions like (7) the mind. Having renounced the five functions of seeing etc, there are however initial and sustained thought and resolve; [65] (9) having renounced receiving (*sampaṭicchana*) and examining (*santīraṇa*) because of that effort; (7) having renounced adverting and examining there is rapture (*pīti*); having abandoned avoidance of boundless sates[66]

[59] See the *citta-niyāma* in the *Atthasālinī*

[60] My translation of the whole passage in curly brackets is tentative – it requires a detailed knowledge of *abhidhamma* categories and idiom that I don't possess. However, compare the discussion of the *cittaniyāma* in the *Atthasālinī* above. The numbers in parentheses don't seem to grammatically fit into the text, so I have not tried to translate them as such – they may be footnotes or references to the *mātika*. The resulting translation doesn't always make sense, and I suspect it wouldn't without considerable study of the *Abhidhamma* more generally, but I'm not very concerned as long as it is understood that what is being discussed is a complex Abhidhamma model of cognition. If we understand this whole passage as saying the *citta-niyāma* refers to the *process of cognition* we'll be on the right track.

[61] Theravāda *Abhidhamma* lists 89 kinds of *cetas*.

[62] *Ekakiccaṭṭhānāni* i.e. *eka-kicca-ṭṭhāna* in the nominative or accusative plural (*–āni*) the places with a single function

[63] *pubbe vuttāni* – "mentioned previously in the commentary"? I am unsure about this.

[64] In this context the five physical senses are referred to as doors (*dvāra*).

[65] *Vitakka-vicāra-adhimokkhā*: This seems to refer to withdrawing from the physical senses in meditation.

[66] I.e. the four boundless states or the *brāhmaviharas*: *mettā*, *karuṇā*, *mudita*, *upekkha*.

and abstinence[67] together with examining, however, (20) and skilful (*kusala*) and indeterminate (*avyākata*) [actions][68] and desire (*chanda*) and examining (*santīraṇa*) ; (5) abandoning sense objects because of boundless; (4) with abstinence (*virati*) they make skilful impulses and functions. And because the door of abstinence is just the mind-door, so there is compassion (*karuṇā*) and sympathetic joy (*mudita*). Just in the mind-door is abstention from bad conduct and grasping the concept of a being (*sattapaññattiggahaṇa*[69]). Although the six doors are unskilful, any conceit, jealousy, avarice and misconduct (*māna-issā-macchariya-kukkuccāni*) come from the mind-door[70]. What is left concerns the six doors and freedom from doors. The remainder is just like the mind. That comprising sense objects will be clearly protected on three grounds.[71]}

---

[67] Probably a reference to abstinence from unskilful actions of body, speech and mind.

[68] *Kusalāvyakatā*. I'm reading it as a *dvandva* compound, i.e. "skilful & indeterminate" (two of the three kinds of mental state, with the third being unskilful "*akusala*" represented by *chando*) but in fact it doesn't really make sense to exclude skilful actions here so I suspect I am confused. Perhaps all mental states are to be rejected?

[69] For *sattapaññatti* "the concept of the being" see SN IV.39 which says that a "concept of being" exists when there is sense object, sense faculty, and sense discrimination, and things to be discriminated by sense discrimination (e.g. *cakkhuviññāṇaviññātabbā dhammā*).

[70] I'm unsure about how to read *manodvārikānevāti*

[71] I'm unsure how to read *parittārammaṇattike* – but it is probably *paritta-ārammaṇa-(t)tike* (protect-conditions-three) in the accusative plural

Niyāma Sutta Translations

Āvaraṇa Sutta

Discourse on Obstructions (AN 6. 86)

Listening to the excellent teachings, [a person] endowed with six things is incompetent to come upon inevitability (*niyāma*) of perfection amongst skilful states:[72] endowed with an obstruction[73] by actions (*kamma*), an obstruction by defilements (*kilesas*), an obstruction by results [of former actions]; with a lack of faith (*saddha*), a lack of zeal (*chandika*), and foolishness (*duppañña*).

Listening to the good teachings, [a person] endowed with six things is competent to come upon inevitability of perfection amongst skilful states: not endowed with an obstruction by actions (*kamma*), nor an obstruction by defilements (*kilesas*), nor an obstruction by results [of former actions]; with faith, zeal, and intelligence (*paññavant*).

---

[72] This sentence is interesting for using *dhamma* in three different senses: things or list items; the teachings (*saddhamma*); and skilful [mental] states. The phrase 'come upon inevitability of perfection amongst skilful states' (*niyāmaṃ okkamituṃ kusalesu dhammesu sammattaṃ*) is a pericope or stock phrase and occurs in all the related *Aṅguttara* texts. Clearly it is related to phrase found in SN 25.1 "entering the inevitability of perfection" (*okkanto sammattaṃ-niyāma*). The verb *okkamati* (infinitive *okkamitum*, present participle *okkanto*) is from the root √*kam* "to go" with the suffix *o-* "down" (= *ava-* c.f. *avakkamati*) and means "enter, fall into (as sleep), develop, to appear in (of a subjective state); to approach". In conjunction with *niyāma* it means "come to inevitability, fall into an assured state" and in these texts the inevitability is with reference to perfection "*sammatta*" (an abstract noun from *sammā* 'right, correct, perfect') which is frequently associated with the limbs of the Eightfold Path. It seems to be something like "confirmed confidence" *aveccappassāda*; else it relates to the idea that there is a point of no return beyond which progress is assured (*sotapanna*) c.f. SN 25.1.

[73] Pāli *āvaraṇatā* literally "a state of obstruction".

Paccaya Sutta

Discourse on Conditions (SN 12.20)

Dwelling at Sāvathī etc.[74] "Bhikkhus, I will teach you dependent arising, and dependently arisen phenomena. Listen to this, make your mind receptive and I will speak."

"Yes, Bhante," the bhikkhus agreed.

The Bhagavan said "Bhikkhus what is dependent arising? 'With birth as condition, there is old age and death.' Whether *tathāgatas* arise or not, this element [of conditionality] is persistent[75], *dhammas*[76]persist [in the presence of their condition] (*dhamma-ṭṭhitatā*[77]), *dhammas* are constrained [by the condition] (*dhamma-niyāmatā*)[78], and specific conditionality (*idappacchayatā*).[79] A tathāgata awakens to the highest

---

[74] The details are missing, but most of this *saṃyutta* are delivered in Jeta Grove of Anāthapiṇḍika's park outside Sāvathī. See especially SN 12.1, which also gives the full version of the *nidāna* chain that is abbreviated in this text.

[75] Pāli *ṭhita* "standing, remaining".

[76] One thing to keep in mind here is that though we call the twelve items in the list "*nidānas*", in Pāli they are actually *dhammas*. *Nidāna* "basis" describes the relationship between these twelve *dhammas*.

[77] Pāli *ṭhitatā* "state or fact of standing or remaining; constancy." The initial *ṭh* becomes *–ṭṭh* in compounds. Buddhaghosa sees *dhamma-* here as plural i.e. "mental objects"; and tells us that conditionally arisen dhammas persist with that condition (*paccayena hi paccayuppannā dhammā tiṭṭhanti* SNA 2.40), i.e. as long as the condition persists. Confusingly Buddhaghosa commenting on the parallel phrase at AN 3.134 glosses *dhamma-* with *sabhāva* "nature; state of mind; truth, reality", most likely meaning "nature" (ANA 2.380). I can't reconcile the two approaches.

[78] Buddhaghosa says here that *dhammaniyāma* refers to the way that "the condition constrains the dhammas [that arise]" (*paccayo dhamme niyāmeti* SA 2.40). Note again *dhammas* in the plural. MN I.259 explores this quality from the other side: "From whatever condition cognition arises, it is known as that kind of consciousness" (*yaññadeva, bhikkhave, paccayaṃ paṭicca uppajjati viññāṇaṃ tena ten'eva saṅkhaṃ gacchati*). Pāli Buddhism makes no allowance for synaesthesia: eye forms and eye faculty only give rise to eye consciousness; never to ear, nose, tongue, or body consciousness. This is a constraint (*niyāma*) of the Buddhist process of cognition.

[79] On these four adjectives see the essay on *dhammaniyāmatā* and *idappacchayatā*, later in this volume.

knowledge and realises this, then tells, teaches, declares, establishes, reveals, analyses, and makes it evident."

And he said, "You should see that with birth as condition there is old age and death."

"With becoming as condition there is birth etc.; with grasping as condition there is becoming etc.; with craving as condition there is grasping etc.; with feeling as condition there is craving etc.; with contact as condition there is feeling etc; with the six sense spheres as condition there is contact etc.; with name and form as condition there are the six sense spheres etc.; with cognition as condition there is name and form etc.; with constructions as condition there is cognition etc.; ignorance as condition there are constructions. Whether *tathāgatas* arise or not, this element [of conditionality] is persistent, *dhammas* persist [in the presence of their condition], *dhammas* are constrained [by the condition], and specific conditionality. A *tathāgata* awakens to the highest knowledge and realises this, then tells, teaches, declares, establishes, reveals, analyses, and makes it evident."

And he said, "You should see that with ignorance as condition there are constructions."

"Thus indeed, bhikkhus, these [conditions][80] have thusness[81], persistence[82], fidelity[83], and specificity[84]; and this is called dependent arising."

---

[80] Thus Buddhaghosa reads *yā tatra*. (SNA 2.41)

[81] Pāli *tathatā* "thusness" (*tatha* + *tā*) according to Buddhaghosa is "from whatever condition, neither more or less, that *dhamma* is produced" insists on the relationship between the condition and the *dhamma* produced. This is the counterpart of *ṭhita* from the previous set of four.

[82] Pāli *avitathatā*, the state of *avitatha*; from *vitatha* (*vi* + *tatha*) no-truth; the double negative makes the basic meaning of *avithata* "truth". Buddhaghosa interprets: "while the necessary conditions come together, there is no non-production or non-existence of existing dhammas, even for a moment." In relation to the earlier adjectives this is related to *dhammaṭṭhitatā* "the persistence of dhammas".

[83] Pāli *anaññathatā* "not otherness" or "without error". Buddhaghosa "*dhammas* are not produced from the conditions of other *dhammas*" i.e. one set of conditions must give rise to the appropriate *dhamma* and no other; likewise a *dhamma* cannot arise from another set of conditions. This is the counterpart of *dhammaniyāmatā* the constraint of *dhammas*.

"And what, bhikkhus, are dependently arisen dhammas? Ageing & death, bhikkhus is impermanent, constructed and dependently arisen[85], its nature is to decay, to perish, to fade to cease.[86] So to birth, becoming, attachment, craving, sensation, contact, the six sense spheres, name & form, cognition, constructs and ignorance."

"Since the ideal disciple[87] sees well, with perfect understanding as they are 'this is dependent arising, these are dependently arisen dhammas'—

—it's not possible that they will run to the past: "I existed in the past; I didn't exist in the past; what was I in the past, why[88] was I in the past; having been what, what was I in the past?"

— it's not possible that they will run to the future: "I will exist in the future; I won't exist in the future; what will I be in the future, why will I be in the future; having been what, what I become in the future?"

— it's not possible that in the immediate present there will be inward doubt: "do I exist; do I not exist; what am I; why am I; where is this being from; where will it go in the future?"

---

[84] Pāli *idappacchayatā* specific conditionality. From *idaṃ paccaya*—PED "having its foundation in this", i.e. "having *this* as a condition" or "having a specific condition". Buddhaghosa is a little cryptic here: "from the condition of ageing & death etc., or from the removal of the condition." I differ from Bodhi on how to interpret this passage (see *Paccaya Sutta Commentary* and my essay later in the book). Here I think the idea is that when the condition is present the *dhamma* arises, and when the condition ceases the *dhamma* ceases.

[85] Pāli *aniccaṃ saṅkhataṃ paṭiccasamuppannaṃ*.

[86] Pāli *khayadhammaṃ vayadhammaṃ virāgadhammaṃ nirodhadhammaṃ*. Note that *–dhamma* here means "nature" so more literally "of a nature to be cut off, of a nature to perish, of a nature to wane, of a nature to cease".

[87] Pāli *ariyasāvaka*.

[88] Pāli *kathaṃ* is often "how?", but it can also mean "why?", "For what reason?" which makes more sense here.

Paccaya Sutta Commentary

Extract from Buddhaghosa's Commentary on the *Paccaya Sutta* (SNA 2.40). Words from the text being commented on are in bold

Iti kho, bhikkhave means "thus indeed bhikkhus." **These** (*yā tatrā*) from amongst [the list of conditions] "with birth as a condition there is ageing and death" etc.; **thusness** (*tathatā*) etc. are synonyms for the mode of conditions: **thusness** (*tathatā*) means that from whatever condition, neither more or less, that *dhamma* is produced; **persistence** (*avitathatā*) means that while the necessary conditions come together, there is no non-production or non-existence of existing dhammas, even for a moment; **fidelity** (*anaññatha*) means that *dhammas* are not produced from the conditions of other *dhammas*; **specificity** (*idapaccayatā*) means from the condition of ageing & death etc., or from the removal of the condition.[89]

---

[89] PED suggests that the use of "group", per Kern, here is wrong, c.f. Bodhi's reading "conditions taken as a group (*paccayasamūhto*)" (2000: 742, n.54). On the face of it *samūhata* is a pp. of *samūhanati* "remove, abolish" (its etymology is *saṃ* + *ud* + √*han* or *saṃ* + *ava* + √*han*; √*han* "smite, strike"). This is confirmed by Buddhist Hybrid Sanskrit forms in BHSD. Compare PED *samūha* "crowd"; and *samūheti* "to gather, collect". PED says *samūheti* is a causative of *saṃ* + √*vah* or √*uh*; but the indicative form (*samuhati*? *saṃvahati*?; c.f. Skt. *saṃ*√*vah* in MW) does not occur in PED, or in the texts. BHSD sv. *samūhati* sees any connection between *samūhati* and *samūha* as "implausible". In short, though Bodhi's reading makes sense, it is implausible on linguistic grounds. Instead we need to think in terms that while the conditions are present the *dhamma* is produced (*imasmiṃ sati, idam hoti*) but when the conditions cease so does the *dhamma* (*imassa nirodhā idaṃ nirujjhati*). This also makes sense, and conforms to Pāli morphology.

Uppādā Sutta

Discourse on Arising (AN 3.134)[90]

Whether *tathāgatas* arise or not, this element of constancy of nature (*dhammaṭṭhitatā*[91]), of the inevitability of nature (*dhamma-niyāmatā*) remains[92]:

All constructs are impermanent.[93]
All constructs are disappointing.[94]
All mental events are insubstantial.[95]

A tathāgata awakens to the highest knowledge and realises this, then tells, teaches, declares, establishes, reveals, analyses, and makes evident:

All constructs are impermanent.
All constructs are disappointing.
All mental events are insubstantial.

---

[90] Numbered 3.137 in CST.

[91] AA glosses *dhamma* with *sabhāva* "nature; state of mind; truth, reality", and where they crossover is in the sense of "nature". This does not mean nature in the general, Romantic sense, as the outdoors, but nature as in the nature of experience. The three *lakkhaṇas* describe important aspects of the nature of experience. Pāli *ṭhita* "standing, remaining"; *ṭhitatā* "state or fact of standing or remaining; constancy." [the *ṭh* becomes *–ṭṭha* in compounds]

[92] Compare SN 12.20 which adds "specific conditionality" (*idappacchayatā*) to the first two qualities and applies them to dependent arising (*paṭiccasamuppādaṃ*) and dependently arisen dhammas (*paṭiccasamuppannā dhammā*). We could say that *dhammaṭṭhitatā*, *dhammaniyāmatā*, are the nature of experience; whereas the *lakkhaṇas* are consequence of that nature.

[93] *sabbe saṅkhārā anicca*. C.f. Dhp. 277-279.

[94] *sabbe saṅkhārā dukkha*

[95] *sabbe dhammā anattā*

Cakkhu Sutta

Discourse on the Eye (SN 25.1)[96]

Based at Sāvathī.[97]

"Bhikkhus, the eye is impermanent (*anicca*), changeable (*vipariṇāma*[98]), and capricious (*aññathābhāvi*[99]); the ear, the tongue, the nose, the body and the mind are impermanent, changeable, and capricious."

"The one who believes in, and is drawn to these facts (*dhammā*) is called 'a believer' (*sassānusārin*[100]), and develops the inevitability of perfection (*sammatta-niyāma*[101]), rising to the level of a superior person, having surpassed the level of ordinary people. It's impossible that they could act in such a way as to be reborn in hell, an animal womb, or the

---

[96] The subsequent *suttas* in this *nikāya* apply precisely the same analysis to forms, sense cognition, contact, sensations, perceptions, intentions, craving, the elements, and the *khandhas*.

[97] Texts in this *Nikāya* often lack the conventional opening and closing statements. Here it just says: *sāvathinidānaṃ*

[98] Or perhaps *vipariṇāminī*, a denominative verb from *vipariṇāma* "changing for the worse, vicissitude".

[99] Or perhaps *aññathābhāvinī*: from *aññathā* "otherwise, otherness" and *bhāvinī* "future" ultimately from *bhāveti* (the causative form of √*bhū*) "beget, produce, increase, cultivate".

[100] Or more literally "one who follows [the teacher] out of faith".

[101] Bodhi (2000: 1004) "one who has entered the fixed course of righteousness". Here Buddhaghosa glosses the term *sammatta-niyāma* as "entering the noble [eight-fold] path" (SNA 2.346). DN III.255 lists eight *sammattas* which equate with the eight limbs of the *ariyamagga*. *Sammatta* is an abstract from *sammā* "right, properly; perfect" which world is used with each limb: e.g. *sammādiṭṭhi* "perfect vision" etc; and therefore means "perfection". Presumably the idea of a "fixed course" derives from the idea that the person becomes a stream-entrant and cannot be reborn in the lower realms. We can see this as a variation on the theme of "reaping what we sow", i.e. inevitability of the result, here applied to the eight-fold path. This could be a "fixed course", but really it's just another kind of necessity or inevitability. Woodward, for once, does better than those who come afterwards with "assurance of perfection" (Vol. 3, p.177).

ghost realm[102]; and it's impossible to die without having personally experienced the fruits of stream-entry."

"For the intelligent one who approves of just these facts because of his measure of insight is called someone who conforms to the facts,[103]

[102] Respectively these are *niraya*, *tiracchāna-yoni*, and *pettivisaya*. The last is a modified form of the afterlife destination of a simple binary rebirth eschatology. In Sanskrit *preta* simply means "the departed" (i.e. the recently dead) and its etymology seems to combine the word for father *pitṛ* since the dead went to the realm of the fathers; and the verb *pra√ī* "gone before, departed". Since the spirits of the dead did not cease to exist, but dwelt in the realm of the fathers for a long time before coming back to earth, such spirits were considered to be a living presence. Brahmins would offer sacrifices to the fathers to sustain them in the afterlife. This afterlife destination appears to be referred to in Buddhist texts as "the other world" (*paraloka*). Buddhists made a parody of these spirits, depicting them as always hungry spirits unable to be satisfied, thus at the same time mocking the practice of sacrifice and ancestor worship. Gananath Obeyesekere (2002) has explored the way this simple eschatology changes under the influence of moral ideas. The first thing that happens is that the afterlife destination bifurcates into places of reward and punishment. Since the upwards direction was traditionally seen as good, the destination for wrong doers was in the downwards direction, hence the name: *niraya* = *nir* (down) + √*ī* "going". (Compare the description of judgement and torture in the *Devadūta Sutta*, MN 130) The word translated as "animal" is *tiracchāna* which is literally "one who goes horizontally" i.e. as opposed to upright like a human.

and enters the inevitability of perfection, rising to the level of a superior person, having surpassed the level of ordinary people. It's impossible that they could act in such a way as to be reborn in hell, an animal womb, or the ghost realm; and it's impossible to die without having personally experienced the fruits of stream-entry."

One who thus understands these facts and sees them thus is called a stream-entrant (*sotāpanna*), constrained to proceed towards full awakening without suffering states of ruin[104].

---

[103] This sentence contains considerable ambiguity and has thus produced various translations, none of which are analysed by the translators: Woodward, in Rhys Davids and Woodward (1917-30: 3.177) "He, brethren, by who these doctrines by his insight are moderately approved"; Bodhi (2000: 1004) "One for whom these teachings are accepted thus after being pondered to a sufficient degree with wisdom..."; Thanissaro "One who after pondering with a modicum of discernment, has accepted that these phenomena are this way"; Piya Tan (2005) "...one who accepts these truths after pondering over them with some wisdom thus". Pāli *Yassa kho, bhikkhave, ime dhammā evaṃ paññāya mattaso nijjhānaṃ khamanti, ayaṃ vuccati 'dhammānusārī'* (*dhammānusārin* is often translated as a Dhamma-devotee or Dhamma-follower). SNA takes *mattaso nijjhānaṃ khamanti* as a unit and glosses it with *pamāṇato olokanaṃ khamanti* which is no easier to translate! The ablative indicates the point of origin of the action so *mattaso... khamanti* "they accept... from a measure"; which suggests "they accept from a measure of insight (*nijjhāna*)". However PED notes that combinations of *nijjhāna* and *khamati* often mean "finds pleasure in", and that *mattaso* often functions adverbially 'in moderation, doing moderately'. The case of the word *paññāya* is ambiguous so it is variously rendered "with wisdom"; "of discernment"; "with some wisdom"; I'm inclined to think that it goes with *yassa*. Woodward's translation mistakenly has "walker in faith" for *dhammānusārin* in 25.1-10. SṬ glosses *olokana* as "seeing constructs with comprehension of the truth" (*saccābhisamaya-saṅkhātaṃ dassanaṃ*); and *khamanti* as "they overcome, bear, they are able" (*sahanti*) and "they are true, they are fit" (*ñāyantī*).

[104] Pāli *a-vinipāta-dhammo niyato*. *Niyata* is the past participle from *ni*$\sqrt{}$*yam* (the verb from which *niyāma* also derives) and literally means "held back"; *vinipāta* is a "ruin or punishment" and *dhamma* here means "a state"; and *avinipātadhamma* is "not in a state of punishment" or "without a state of punishment". Bodhi translates *niyato* "fixed in destiny" which reflects the idea that the stream-entrant is bound to awaken. Thanissaro changes from "orderly" above, and here opts for "steadfast" which seems to miss the point.

Essays

These essays were originally written as standalone pieces of writing for my blog. As such there is some repetition, especially in the introductions.

Dharma-niyama in the Vyākaraṇa-Mahābhāṣya

The term "dharma-niyama" has taken on increased significance in the Triratna movement over the last few years.[105] In 2010, Dharmacari Subhuti circulated an article—*Revering and Relying on the Dharma*—which emerged from his conversations with Sangharakshita on the subject. The paper expounded a metaphysics and cosmology based on Sangharakshita's notion of *niyāma*, i.e. that of a universe consisting of a layered hierarchy of "orders of conditionality" in which different layers of reality are controlled by their own *niyama*. Sangharakshita's conception of "The Dharma niyama" was further refined in Subhuti's essay "A Supra-Personal Force" (2012), "*the Dharma-niyāma* is the kind of conditionality that comes into play when one sees the Dharma directly for oneself, especially by breaking free of the illusion of a separate selfhood" (2012: 4).

In the day to day discourse of the Order one now frequently hears reference to "the Dharma niyama" (with capital Dh) translated by Subhuti as "transcendental order" in the place that used to be occupied by phrases drawn from German Idealism, such as "the Transcendental" and "the Absolute".[106] In *A Survey of Buddhism*, a book that continues to be foundational for the Triratna Order, Sangharakshita speaks of wisdom as "a direct, non-conceptual apprehension of transcendental Reality" (1993: 25). He later backed away from the use of idealist terminology and suggested that his use of them was misunderstood. In which case, it seems that in reifying the term "the dharma-niyama"—

---

[105] In this essay I take "dhamma" and "niyama" to be anglicised words unless specifically quoting a passage in Pāli or Sanskrit. However, note that in Triratna we tend to (tacitly) base our Anglicisation on the Sanskrit spelling *dharma* rather than the Pāli *dhamma*.

[106] Sangharakshita's sources for these terms are uncertain but amongst Buddhist authors who we know influenced him they were used frequently by D. T Suzuki and Edward Conze, both heavily influenced by Theosophy (where the terms are also used frequently).

indicated by the use of the definite article and the idea of it being a "supra-personal force"—we may have once again misunderstood him.

The suggestion that these kinds of terms in Sangharakshita's lexicon represent a tendency to eternalism in this thinking about Buddhism continues to crop up from time to time.[107] While we have trenchant critiques of scientific rationalism and some understanding of how we are influenced by Protestantism, the Triratna Order seems reluctant to confront the major influence it takes from Romanticism.[108] Indeed I think few in the Order would even view this influence as problematic were it to be acknowledged.

Just before Subhuti made known Sangharakshita's new thinking on *niyāma*, a side discussion was started up in the order by one of my colleagues. Dhīvan circulated a long essay "Sangharakshita, the Five Niyamas and the Problem of Karma" (2009), which argued that Sangharakshita's use of the term niyama was, in fact, an innovation and not based, as was claimed, on a traditional interpretation. He showed how the idea of *niyama* developed from the 5th century commentarial literature where it first occurred, through the interpretative lenses of Ledi Sayadaw and particularly Caroline Rhys Davids. The latter was an influence on Sangharakshita in many ways. Dhīvan argued that though Sangharakshita was largely drawing on Rhys Davids rather than canonical texts, his doctrinal innovation was both justified and necessary in light of, and successful in responding to, the concerns of his followers. According to Dhīvan, the so-called "five niyamas" teaching is authentically Dharmic, just not traditional. One of the main differences of opinion was the meaning of the word "niyama".

[107] The two Order members who openly argued this line during my time in the Order have both since resigned.

[108] German Idealist philosophy, particularly that of Freidrich Schlegel, Freidrich Schelling, and Johann Wolfgang von Goethe played a central role in the English Romantic movement via Samuel Coleridge who promoted their ideas in England. On the role of these major strands of modernism in the formation of contemporary forms of Buddhism see McMahan (2008). It is unfortunate that McMahan ignores liberalism, a major strand of modernism. Ṭhanissaro's (2015) book *Buddhist Romanticism* takes up the theme but the author is an apologist for modern Theravāda and sometimes appears to consider all non-traditional thought to be romanticism.

> "However, according to my understanding of the Pāli language and the Theravādin commentarial tradition, the word niyama does not mean what Sangharakshita or Subhuti take it to mean, and Sangharakshita's list of five niyamas is a creative re-interpretation of Mrs Rhys-Davids' creative misinterpretation of what the commentators say" (Dhīvan 2013).

Sangharakshita, following Sayadaw and/or Rhys Davids, takes niyama to mean "order of conditionality". The set of five niyamas are said to correspond to five "orders of conditionality" i.e. five hierarchical domains in which conditionality operates. However, niyama simply does not and cannot mean "order", it means "limit, restriction, constrain; inevitability". Dhivan's work had little impact in the Order and no discernible impact on Sangharakshita or Subhuti. And to the best of my knowledge, this has not changed.

I joined this discussion in 2012 when I began circulating drafts of the translations in this book. In producing these translations it became clear that Dhīvan's comments regarding the relation to the tradition were accurate. Part of the problem was that the texts were not easy to access for non-Pāli readers. Sayadaw had translated the *Atthasālinī* in 1965 (republished 1978) and Walpola Rahula translated the *Sumaṅgalavilāsinī* in 1974. Sayadaw's translation is widely available on the internet and was used by Subhuti in his exposition. However, Sayadaw translates in such a way as to support his modern reinterpretation of the *niyamas* and often with no reference to the actual Pāli usage. Problems with Sayadaw's translation are dealt with in my translation notes and in Dhīvan's essay and article (see bibliography under both Dhīvan and Jones).

While the word *niyama* (or *niyāma*, the two spellings are interchangeable in Pāli despite deriving differently) occurs in sutta texts, it is not until the fifth century CE that Buddhaghosa takes up the word to produce the five categories that form the basis of Sangharakshita's metaphysics. The translation that follows shows how the word *dharma-niyama* was used in Classical Sanskrit by the grammarian Patañjali commenting on Pāṇini's descriptive grammar, the *Aṣṭādhyāyī*.[109] Patañjali's *Vyākaraṇa-Mahābhāṣya* or *Major Commentary on Grammar* is usually dated to ca. 150 BCE, though this date is somewhat uncertain. In the passage concerned, Patañjali is commenting on some glosses on the *Aṣṭādhyāyī* found in the *Vārttika*, a commentary by Kātyāyana. This whole section from the introduction to the *Mahābhāṣya* concerns the relationship between meaning (*artha*) and words (*śabda*).

This translation is intended for my use and ought to be treated with some suspicion or at least read in conjunction with the published translation by Joshi and Roodbergen. My translation relies on the published translation and comments made during our class reading of the text.

Vyākaraṇa-Mahābhāṣya

Paspaśāhnika (p.7-8)[110]

[7] {80} But how is it known that the connection between a meaning and a word is established (*siddha*)?

From the world (*lokataḥ*) [i.e. from people in the world].

{81: 198} In the world, having acquired [in the mind] a thing meant (*artha*) the words (*śabdān*) are uttered. They make no effort in accomplishing this. However, an effort is required to accomplish a thing that needs to be made. For example: wanting to do a job with [or requiring] a pot, he goes to the house of a potter as says "Make a pot (*kuru ghaṭaṃ*), I require it for a job". On the contrary, one who will be using words doesn't go to the house of a grammarian and

---

[109] The name Patañjali is also associated with the *Yogasūtras* but the works are so different in content, style, and idiom that many scholars find it difficult to see them as the work of the same person as the work on grammar.

[110] Numbers in square brackets refer to the page numbers of the Sanskrit edition by Keilhorn (3rd ed. 1962). Numbers in curly brackets refer to section and page numbers in the translation by Joshi & Roodbergen. Passages in **bold** are Patñjali's citations from the *Vārttika* by Kātyāyana.

say [8] "Make words, I will utter them." Right away having acquired the thing meant, he utters the words.

{82} So, if the world is an authority (*pramāṇa*) in this [matter] what is the use of grammar?

Where the use of a word is connected to the meaning from the world [as authority], grammar provides a restriction for the sake of religious merit (*dharma-niyama*).

{83: 200} Where the use of a word is connected to the meaning from the world [as authority], grammar provides a restriction for the sake of religious merit. What is *dharma-niyama*? It is a restriction for Dharma (*dharmāya niyamaḥ*); or, a restriction for the purpose of Dharma (*dharmārthaḥ vā niyamaḥ*); or a restriction aiming at Dharma (*dharmaprayojanaḥ vā niyamaḥ*)

Just as [in the case of] secular and Vedic [precepts].

{84: 202} The southerners have a preference for *taddhita* compounds. [111] So they say '*laukikeṣu*' and '*vaidikeṣu*' [in what is related to the world and what is related to the Vedas] instead of '*loke*' and '*vede*' [in the world and in the Vedas].

Or rather, the meaning of the *taddhita* is appropriate, i.e. just as the precepts (*kṛtānta*) found in secular and Vedic texts. So far as the world is concerned it is said: "a domestic rooster is not to be eaten; a domestic pig is not to be eaten." And that which is to be eaten is taken to remove hunger. And one is also able to remove hunger by eating dog meat. In this case, a restriction (*niyama*) is made: this is to be eaten; this is not to be eaten.

In the same way, there is desire for women because of sexual arousal. And the satisfaction of sexual arousal may be gained equally from available and unavailable [women]. In

---

[111] *Taddhita* compounds are usually made by adding suffixes to a verbal root, which is usually accompanied by lengthening of the root vowel. In this case, *laukika* comes from the noun *loka*, with the suffix *–ka* and lengthening the root vowel from *o* to *au*; lokikeṣu is the locative case.

this case, a restriction is made: she is available; she is unavailable.

{85: 207} Indeed in the Vedas also it is said "a Brahmin takes the vow (*vrata*) of milk (*payo*), a king the vow of gruel (*yavāgū*) and the merchant the vow of curds (*āmikṣā*)" And that "vow" is taken for the purpose of taking food (*abhyavahāra*). It is possible to take a rice (*śāli*) or meat (*māṃsa*) vow etc, as well. In this case, a restriction is made.

Similarly, it is said "The sacrificial post (*yūpa*) should be made of bilva or khādira wood. "Sacrificial post" is taken to mean what the [sacrificial] animal is tied to. And by this, an animal might be tied to any bit of timber, erected or not erected. In this case, a restriction is made.

Similarly, the potsherds (*kapālāni*) are placed by the fire and the mantra is chanted "*bhṛgūṇām aṅgirasām gharmasya tapasā tapyadhvam*" [be heated by the heat of Bhṛgu and Aṅgirasa]. Even without the mantra, fire whose action is to burn would heat those potsherds. In this case, a restriction is made: "done this way it leads to bliss (*abhyudaya*) [i.e. to heaven]."

{86:208} Thus here also the understanding of meaning may equally be expressed by correct words (*śabda*) and incorrect words (*apaśabda*) a restriction for the purposes of religious merit is made. "The meaning is only to be expressed by corrects words not by incorrect words. Done this way it leads to bliss."

Comments

According to the commentaries ancient and modern, that *dharma* is being used in the sense of *puṇya* "religious merit". The idea that doing things in the way constrained by the injunctions or precepts (*kṛtānta*) will be a "causer of bliss" (*abhyudayakārin*) confirms this. *Artha* may have the sense of "referent" (thing referred to by a word) or "meaning" (the definition of a word) and it's not always clear if Patañjali makes this distinction.

The audience for this text lived their lives according to many religious and secular constraints (*niyāma*). From the text, we can see that some of them make sense on face value and some of them don't. Under most circumstances, it is clear, for example, who is an available sexual partner and who isn't, even in our rather wanton society. In ancient India, it was probably even more obvious since a person's spouse was the only sanctioned sexual partner, although prostitutes did ply their trade.

It might not be so obvious why a domestic pig was not appropriate food. The precept allows wild pigs to be eaten. This is partly the point. A negative precept that says "don't eat domestic pigs" is specific. We might be tempted to take the general corollary that *everything else* is OK to eat. We might, for example, decide that dog meat was OK. However, in India, as in the modern west, there was an unspoken understanding that dog meat was not for human consumption. There is no natural reason that this is so. Dog meat is consumed in some parts of the world and is presumably no more prone to disease or no less nourishing than any other kind of meat. We just don't eat dog and may even feel a sense of disgust at the thought. There is an implied restriction in the background to the specific restriction.

As mentioned above, one of the points of controversy in Dhīvan's initial essays on the *niyāmas* was over the meaning of the word. In this text, there is no doubt that it simply means "restriction". One *could* eat anything, but there are various kinds of restrictions on what one *may* eat. One *could* have sex with anyone but, in practice, one has a limited choice of partners. However, the specific term *dharma-niyama* means a restriction for the sake of religious merit. That is to say that it is an injunction whose authority stems from the Vedas and is ultimately aimed at a good rebirth or liberation through the correct performance of religious rituals.

Fundamentally, this argument is about restrictions on what constitutes a correct word (*śabda*) and what is an incorrect word (*apaśabda*). Pragmatically Patañjali has to admit that many non-standard words are in common use. He is arguing that despite the many choices of words, that some are better than others are. In particular, he is arguing for what we call the Classical Sanskrit forms sanctioned by Pāṇini as correct and dialectical variations as incorrect. Here he points out even though we always have many choices of how to behave, that various kinds of restrictions apply: secular or worldly restrictions (*laukikā*) and religious restrictions (v*aidikā*) found in the Vedic texts. Words are also restricted by secular and religious usage.

This is not so different from our time and place. Most people would use a different mode of speech when having fun with their friends than they might at a job interview. For English speakers in Britain, the issue of local dialect words and expressions is a common one. At present, the mood seems to be going against allowing children to use dialect at school for fear that they won't be able to distinguish different contexts as adults and might use the wrong mode of speech.[112] In other words, social liberals fear that those whose dialect differs from the standard will be socially disadvantaged (which is historically the case in the UK).

For the Buddhist who is interested in the concept of niyama, the import is clear. Niyama means "constraint, restriction, limitation or inevitability". It is about restricted choices, vows made, and precepts imposed; or in the jargon of moral philosophy about a deontological approach to morality. In the Pali texts, niyama refers to the restrictions on how change occurs, to the inevitability of certain events, and to the fixed course of evolution of those types of events. Things change, but not randomly. Plant a rice grain and it can only grow into a rice plant, and no other kind of plant. Perform an evil action and it inevitably ripens as a painful *vedanā* (which requires one to have a body capable of experiencing *vedanā*).

In the case of *dhamma-niyama,* it is used by the Buddhist tradition to explain the series of miraculous events that accompany the birth of a Buddha. There is a restriction on the universe related to the life history of a Buddha. As it says in the *Sumaṅgalavilāsinī* (DNA 2.431):

> "The shaking of the 10,000 world system when the *bodhisatta* enters his mother's belly and other such phenomena [associated with the life story of the Buddha as

112

> told in the *Mahāpadāna Sutta*], this is called the fixed course of nature (*dhamma-niyāma*). The fixed course of natures is understood as consisting in this."

Such miracles as occur are bound to occur; they are required for the life story of a Buddha. I have tended to translate *dhamma-niyāma* as "the fixed course of nature", but I might well have translated it here as "a restriction imposed by religion". In other words, this is simply something that Buddhists believe, and, like the audience for Patañjali, they believe it because it is said in a sacred text.

☸

Niyama in the Sāṃkhyakārikā & Buddhaghosa's Commentaries.

This essay will briefly outline some ideas from the *Sāṃkhyakārikā*, the oldest extant text of the ancient Indian worldview known as Sāṃkhya. I will compare this with ideas expressed by Buddhaghosa in the *Sumaṅgalavilāsinī* and the *Atthasālinī*.

We saw, in the previous essay, that the word *niyama* means "restriction" in *śāstric* Sanskrit and here I will reinforce this by showing how the *Sāṃkhyakārikā* uses the word, with a few notes on how this was taken up in the *Yogasūtras* also attributed to Patañjali. In addition, I will note certain similarities between the Sāṃkhya notion of causality and the way that Buddhaghosa uses the word *niyama* to highlight restrictions on the processes of causality.

The *Sāṃkhyakārikā* is a *sūtra*-style text composed ca. 350-450 CE and attributed to Īśvarakṛṣṇa. In Indian literature, *sūtra*-style generally means it is aphoristic, terse, and generally requires a good deal of unpacking. It is partly this general meaning of the word that makes scholars consider the Buddhist use of *sūtra* to translation Pāli *sutta* to be a hyper-Sanskritisation for *sukta*, i.e. *su-ukta* "well uttered", a word used for the verses of the *Ṛgveda*. In any case, the SK outlines the *darśana* or (world)view of the Sāṃkhya school of Indian thought. It is non-Vedic, even critical of the Vedas, and concerned with soteriology. The basic Sāṃkhya view was adapted by Yoga schools, for example, they added Īśvara or god to this originally atheistic (*nāstika*) worldview.

The characteristic idea of Sāṃkhya is a doctrine known as *satkārya* which states that the product of causation already exists in the cause (which is a conjecture similar to Buddhaghosa's *bījaniyāma*). I will say more about this below. The Sāṃkhya world is analysed into a hierarchy of 24 elements or *tattvas,* which are produced when unmanifest nature (*prakṛti*) is disrupted by *puruṣa* (literally "man" but here meaning something like "soul"). What results is the manifest world (*vyaktam*). The 24 elements result from the interactions of three qualities: *sattva* "purity', *rajas* "passion", and *tamas* "darkness". *Kārikā* 12 of the *Sāṃkhyakārikā* gives us an outline of the three *guṇas* that uses the word *niyama*. Here the three *guṇas* or qualities are each said to have a particular essence (*ātmaka*) and a purpose (*artha*).

> The guṇas have the essence of pleasure, pain, and apathy; and the purpose of illumination, activity, and restriction;
>
> And their functions with respect to each other are suppressing, supporting, producing, and forming pairs.[113]

In particular, the guṇa *tamas* or darkness has the purpose of *niyama* "restriction". Kārikā 13 adds that *tamas* is heavy (*guru*) and enveloping or enclosing (*varaṇaka*). The weight and restriction of *tamas* is implicitly contrasted in kārikā 12 with the *pravṛtti* "activity, energy, restlessness" of *rajas*. In the *Yogasūtras* of Patañjali *niyama* takes on an applied meaning of "a vow to be observed", i.e. a voluntary restriction. One of the more popular traditional commentaries on the *Sāṃkhyakārikā*, by Gaudapada, comments here that "Tamas is adapted to restrain, i.e. is competent at fixation." (*niyamārthaṃ tamaḥ sthitau samartham ity artha*). Here *sthiti* "fixing, stopping, halting" is offered as a word with a similar sense (not quite a synonym), i.e. that which restricts the movement of X, causes X to stand still or be fixed. And this is the role of *tamas* that helps us to zero in on how the word *niyama* is used in śāstric Sanskrit.

This way of thinking may well have influenced Buddhaghosa when he composed the fivefold *niyama* not just in the sense of the word itself. Buddhaghosa seems to have some of the same concerns over the limitations of causality that we see in *Sāṃkhyakārikā* 9.

> Because the non-existent cannot be made, because of the grasping of the material basis, and because not all possibilities exist;

---

[113] *prītyapṛitiviṣādātmakāḥ prakāśapravṛttiniyamārthāḥ* |
anyo 'anyābhibhavāśrayajananamithunavṛttiyaśca gunāḥ ||12||

Because the making is possible [only] of what is capable [to be made]; and because of existence in a cause, the product exists.[114]

This is the fundamental statement of the Sāṃkhya idea of causality, *satkāryavāda*, i.e. that the effects already exist in the cause. No causation *ex nihilo* is possible, a substrate (*upādāna*) that contains the outcome is necessary. Things cannot arise haphazardly. Things can only be produced by what is capable of producing them. Whether these reasons necessitate *satkāryavāda* is moot, but these are the supporting arguments given in the *Sāṃkhyakārikā*.

How does this relate to Buddhaghosa? The says *sarvasambhavābhāvāt* "because not all possibilities exist" which means that things cannot arise haphazardly; also *śaktasya śakyakaraṇāt* "because the making is possible [only] of what [the cause] is capable of," which means that a cause is only capable of producing that which it is capable of producing. The same restrictions apply in Buddhaghosa's scheme of conditionality, which insists on a non-random and inevitable relationship between cause and effect. For Buddhaghosa this restriction in a non-random process has the flavour of inevitability. We see in the *Kathāvatthu* debates on *niyāma* that some Buddhists found this acceptance of inevitability problematic because it seemed to be fatalistic or deterministic. This opened the possibility of Buddhist doctrine being confused with Ājivaka doctrine and the *Kathāvatthu* author is at pains to ensure this does not happen (McDermott 1989).

In his use of the word *niyama*, Buddhaghosa emphasises the inevitability of karmic retribution.[115] The inevitable production of *vedanā* by karma (*kamma-niyāma*) is analogous to the natural processes of plants coming to fruition (*bīja-niyāma*) and the arrival of the monsoon rains in season (*utu-niyāma*). The production of cognitions from sense contact was also an analogous process (*citta-niyāma*). In his

---

[114] *asad akaraṇād upādānagrahaṇāt sarvasambhavābhāvāt* | *śaktasya śakyakaraṇāt kāraṇabhāvāc ca sat kāryam.* ||9||

[115] For Buddhaghosa, the inevitability of karma ripening was axiomatic but, as I showed in Attwood (2014), this axiom did not hold across the Buddhist world or over time.

commentarial texts that employ the fivefold niyama, Buddhaghosa spends most time illuminating the process of karma and insisting on the inevitability of it. Actions result in consequences in a non-random way. This is the focus of his use of the concept of niyama. It is what the commentaries insist on. The restriction on *karma* is that the fruits of actions must inevitably ripen. Later Theravāda commentators using the fivefold *niyama* scheme focus more on the production of cognitions.

Restriction and inevitability are two ways of looking at the same thing, one focused on the process and the other on the end-point. If a process can only unfold in a restricted way, then the process follows a fixed course, the outcome is inevitable. If one plants rice seed then the restriction on cause and effect says that only a rice plant can grow from it, or, it is inevitable that a rice plant comes from a rice seed. Buddhaghosa calls this *bīja-niyama* "the restriction on seeds" or "the fixed course of seeds". Elsewhere in the Buddhist world, they began to treat actions as more literally creating seeds that are held in a receptacle (*ālaya*) in some part of the mind (*vijñāna*), but that is another story.

Buddhaghosa adds that the miracles accompanying the main events of the life of a Buddha are said to be of the same type of inevitability as these natural processes (*dhammatā*). They are things that inevitably happen when a Buddha is conceived, born, becomes awakened and dies. This he calls *dhamma-niyama.*

So when Buddhaghosa reads *imasmin sati idaṃ hoti*, he does not see this as optional or contingent on any other fact. For Buddhaghosa there is a restriction on the way causation happens: when the condition is present (*imasmin sati*) then it is inevitable (*niyama*) that the conditioned exists (*idam hoti*). This is particularly so in the case of the restriction on karma (*kamma-niyama*). Having acted, the results of the action follow one *unerringly.* To illustrate this point in the *Sumaṅgalavilāsinī* Buddhaghosa uses the *Dhammapada* verse 127:

Not in the sky, nor the middle of the ocean,
Nor in a mountain cave;
Though terrified there is nowhere on earth,
Where one might escape from an evil action.

Furthermore, in the *Atthasālinī* passage, he expands on this using the commentarial back story to this same verse. In this text, about one half is given over to the discussion of restrictions on *karma*, about one quarter to the restrictions on the processes of the mind, and one quarter to the rest. In both cases, *dhamma-niyama* refers solely to the miraculous events during the life of a Buddha.

At the very least, Īśvarakṛṣṇa, the author of the *Sāṃkhyakārikā,* and Buddhaghosa, author of the *pañcavidho niyamo*, shared an interest in the limitations or restrictions which were observed in relation to causation. Neither author accepted that causation is random or unpredictable. On the contrary, both see the universe as having an order to it that places limitations on how causation and change occur. Buddhaghosa's notion of *utu-niyama* and *bīja-niyama* would have been obvious to Īśvarakṛṣṇa. We too can see that if we plant rice we *must* get a rice plant and not some other species; and that the monsoon does not come at random but at roughly the same time each year. The use of such analogies is widespread in Indian literature.

So if the universe has an order, and that order imposes restrictions on the functioning of conditionality, then is it not acceptable to speak of "orders of conditionality"? I still think this is not the case. What is being described in the texts on *niyāma* is *one process—paṭiccasamuppāda—* that has a number of restrictions on how it works that make the results inevitable and fixed. There is only one order of conditionality in Buddhist doctrine. Intentional actions must reach fruition as rebirth or *vedanā*, and this must happen in timely and appropriate manner.[116] By contrast, in the *Yogasūtras*, *niyama* is often translated as "observance", but it means "a [voluntarily] restriction on behaviour". The five restrictions are cleanliness (*śauca*), contentment (*santoṣa*), austerity (*tapas*), study (*svādhyāya*), and devotion (*praṇidhāna*).

Buddhaghosa's fivefold scheme is neither systematic nor comprehensive. The number five is arbitrary. There is no implied

[116] I have commented at length (Attwood 2018b) on the application of dependent arising to explain karma and concluded that it is not entirely coherent. Karma requires delayed consequences and dependent arising forbids them. This theme is prominent in Nāgārjuna's account of karma.

hierarchy and the niyamas were not always presented in the same order. Though Buddhaghosa himself placed differing emphasis on each of the five aspects, we can see that this emphasis was purely rhetorical. Buddhaghosa was addressing a particular set of problems when he employed this scheme , not speculating about causation more generally. Later Pāli commentaries placed more emphasis on the fixed course of the *cittavithī* i.e. *citta-niyāma.*

Of the five aspects of restricted causation, the seed (*bīja*) and seasonal (*utu*) restrictions the same concepts occur to Īśvarakṛṣṇa. The action (*karma*) and mental (*citta*) restrictions are obvious enough to a person who is well versed in the metaphysics of karma and rebirth and the Buddhist account of cognition. Or perhaps one might argue that they become obvious to anyone willing to examine their experience using Buddhist practices. The dharmic restriction is just something we have to take Buddhaghosa's word for. It is a supernatural belief, and thus not amenable to empirical study. Though it might make an interesting foil to these people who pop up from time to time claiming to be "the second Buddha." If the "10,000 world system" did not shake when you were born, then you are not a Buddha, because this is what *inevitably* happens. And maybe this was part of Buddhaghosa's point?

☸

Niyāma, Caroline Rhys Davids, and British Emergentism.

Dhīvan Thomas Jones (2012) established that Caroline Rhys Davids' interpretation of the Buddhist commentarial concept of *niyāma* was a creative re-interpretation that led to a series of subtle reinterpretations by other commentators. This article presents a circumstantial case that when Caroline Rhys Davids re-interpreted *pañcavidho niyāmo* ("five kinds of constraint") as five branches of a cosmic order that governs the universe, she was employing an idea that she borrowed from the minor school of philosophical thought known as British Emergentism (ca. 1843–1925). The case is circumstantial because Rhys Davids does not cite her European sources, instead, she implies that the interpretation she gives is implicit in Buddhaghosa's commentaries. However, we can present circumstantial evidence to establish that she had the means, motive, and opportunity for this borrowing and synthesis.

The Fivefold Niyāma

The fivefold-*niyāma* is a Buddhist idea about the nature of conditionality, which first appears in Buddhaghosa's fifth-century CE commentaries on the Pāli *Sutta-piṭaka* and *Abhidhamma-piṭaka*. The order in which the kinds of *niyāma* are given is variable, though the interpretation associated with each is stable. In the *Sumaṅgalavilāsinī* (DNA II.432), for example, the order is *kamma-niyāma, utu-niyāma, bīja-niyāma, citta-niyāma*, and *dhamma-niyāma.* In the *Atthasālinī*, a commentary on the *Dhammasaṅgaha*, the order is *bīja, utu, kamma, dhamma, citta*, but they all have the same meanings. A rice seed (*bīja*) is constrained to produce a rice plant; a tree is constrained to flower and fruit in the proper season (*utu*); an action (*kamma*) is constrained to inevitably produce appropriate and timely results; the mind (*citta*) is constrained by the functioning of the mental processes (*cittavīthi*) as conceived by the Theravāda *Abhidhamma*, and the biography of any Buddha is constrained by the natural pattern (*dhamma*) of how the lives of all Buddhas unfold (emphasised by miracles at certain milestones).

Judging by how much space he devoted to each, for Buddhaghosa the primary purpose of *niyāma* was to emphasise the inevitability, the appropriateness, and timeliness of the outcomes of karma. The twelfth- or thirteenth-century Sri Lankan and South Indian commentators were focussed more on the workings of the *cittavīthi*.

Jones notes: "Caroline Rhys Davids introduced the doctrine of *niyāma* to the English-speaking world in her 1912 book *Buddhism: a Study of the Buddhist Norm*" (Jones 2012: 546). In Rhys Davids (1912), *niyāma* represents an impersonal moral order. She outlines the scheme, following the order found in the *Sumaṅgalavilāsinī*, but giving each *niyāma* a modern spin:

> *kamma-niyama*, order of act-and-result; *utu-niyama*, physical (inorganic) order; *bīja-niyama*, order of germs or seeds (physical organic order); *chitta-niyama* [sic], order of mind, or conscious life; *dhamma-niyama*, order of the norm, or the effort of nature to produce a perfect type. (1912: 119)

Like Buddhaghosa, Rhys Davids is focussed on *niyāma* as exemplifying an impersonal, natural, moral order in the universe.

> "Going farther than the modern scientific standpoint, [the early Buddhists] substituted a cosmodicy for a theodicy, a natural moral order for the moral design of a creative deity." (1912: 118-119)

Rhys Davids takes *niyāma* to mean "going on, process" and the abstract form *niyāmatā* as "normal orderly procedure". It is further linked by both Caroline and Thomas Rhys Davids with the idea of "natural law, cosmic order." (Jones 2012: 557). This modern interpretation is quite different from what the ancient commentators intended. *Niyāma*, and the alternative spelling *niyama*, are both used in the senses of "restriction, limit; fixed course, inevitability". Jones explains that, from an etymological point of view, the word means "holding-back" or "restraint". It is used in this sense in Sanskrit, for example in the ethical restraints of the second of the eight limbs of *aṣṭāṅga-yoga*. The Sanskrit word also has the meaning of "necessity," "constraint," or "fixed rule" (Jones 2012: 557). It is in the sense of "necessity" or "constraint" that Buddhaghosa uses the word *niyāma* in his commentarial scheme.

For Rhys Davids, the five-fold *niyāma* scheme represents an imminent moral order inherent in the universe. This moral order is teleological: it leads to the production of a "perfect type" represented by the Buddha (1912: 547-550). Although Rhys Davids was profoundly influenced by rational humanism, we can see in these statements linking morality with teleology, a fundamentally *religious* aspect to her thinking. We can also note that, at least for in Pāli texts that Rhys Davids studied, Buddhists did not see the universe in teleological terms. Of course, the early Buddhists did argue that Buddhists ought to be motivated by the *possibility* of attaining *nirvāṇa*, but they ascribed this possibility to the willed actions of the individual. In the absence of such willed actions, a being would simply cycle around being endlessly reborn. There is no inevitability about liberation in early Buddhist thought or the later Theravāda commentarial tradition. The universe, as the idea of *niyāma* seeks to demonstrate, is an impersonal engine of cause and effect with no particular goal in mind.[117] The universe simply pays out in kind. So that having acted, one could always expect an appropriate and timely consequence.

Subsequently, others used *niyāma* in this sense of "natural order" and developed it. For example, in his 1933 booklet, *Buddhism in a Nutshell*, the Sri Lankan Bhikkhu, Nārada (1982), used the concept of *niyāma* to argue that we cannot ascribe all events to karma as a cause, since, in this interpretation, *kamma-niyāma* is only one of five types of causality. Nārada changed the order to *utu-niyāma*, *bīja-niyāma*, *kamma-niyāma*, *dhamma-niyāma*, and *citta-niyāmai.* He lists several kinds of phenomena which fit into each (Jones 2012: 553). Nārada and

[117] I have argued (Attwood 2012, 2014) that this impersonal moral universe may owe something to Zoroastrianism. The idea sits alongside some other details of early Buddhism, such as treating morality as relating to acts of the triad, body speech and mind, that are difficult to explain except by unlikely coincidence or contact with Zoroastrianism, most likely through groups of migrants.

subsequent interpreters tend to see the five kinds of *niyāma* as five distinct categories, whether of phenomena or causation. This is a further step away from the idea enunciated by Buddhaghosa.

The argument against everything being caused by karma becomes a signature interpretation of *niyāma* and continues to be useful in this context because this teaching is common in Tibetan Buddhist circles. This sense of *niyāma* is also taken up by Kate Crosby (2008) in her exploration of Sri Lankan Buddhist responses to the tsunami of 2004. There are canonical sources, e.g. the *Sivaka Sutta* (SN 36.21), that deny karma as the sole cause of events. However, in his notes on this text Theravādin bhikkhu, Thanissaro, has argued that, since karma is the underlying cause of the circumstances of our birth, even those events not directly caused by karma are indirectly caused by it.

> "However, if we compare this list with his definition of old kamma in SN 35.145, we see that many of the alternative causes are actually the result of past actions.... The point here is that old and new kamma do not override other causal factors operating in the universe — such as those recognized by the physical sciences — but instead find their expression within those factors." (Thanissaro 2005)

In the 1960s, Sangharakshita took up *niyāma* with much the same sense given by Nārada. In his view:

> [not] all experienced effects are products of willed action or karma . . . This important distinction is elaborated in the formula of the five *niyamas*, or different orders of cause-effect or conditionality obtaining in the universe. They are *utu-niyama*, physical inorganic order; *bīja-niyama*, physical organic or biological order; *mano-niyama* (nonvolitional)

> mental order[118]; *karma-niyama*, volitional order; and dharma-niyama, transcendental order. (1967: 69)

Indeed, "Sangharakshita continues this terminological development by introducing the idea that the five kinds of *niyāma* constitute 'different orders of . . . conditionality,' that is, orders of *paṭicca-samuppāda*. He also develops a theme mentioned by Caroline Rhys Davids when he takes *dhamma-niyāma* to mean 'transcendental order'" (Jones 2012: 554), this transcendental order related to what he has called "transcendental Reality" (2009: 256). Later Sangharakshita glossed *dhamma-niyama* as the "sum total of the spiritual laws which govern progress through the stages of the Buddhist path" (1994: 107).

Unlike Darwinians, Rhys Davids and Sangharakshita envisaged a teleological universe evolving a perfect type in the shape of a Buddha (2009: 258). We can further note that Sangharakshita describes his approach to evolution as "very broadly 'vitalist' in that it recognizes a will to Enlightenment somehow present in all forms of life", though he cautions that, "evolution is just a metaphor" just a "temporal model". In his view "self-transcendence, is what the whole of evolution, from the amoeba upward, is all about." (2009: 257-8).

Another influential source for the modern understanding of the *niyāma* doctrine is Ledi Sayadaw's *Niyāmadīpanī*, a commentary on *niyāma* composed in Pali and published in English translation in 1965. The date for the original composition of *Nyāmadīpanī* is unclear:

> "I have not been able to discover the original publication date of Ledi Sayadaw's *Niyāma-dīpanī* or of the correspondence with Mrs. Rhys Davids; however, the translation cites Mrs. Rhys Davids's Buddhism of 1912 and must therefore post-date it, and Ledi Sayadaw died in 1923." (Jones 2012: 575)

---

118 It's not clear why Sangharakshita substitutes *manoniyāma* for *cittaniyāma*; in Buddhaghosa's terminology *citta* here has a specific meaning of one moment in the model of mental processes (*cittavīthi*) adopted in the Theravāda *Abhidhamma* model of perception.

This shows that if anything Ledi Sayadaw was drawing on Rhys Davids, rather than the other way around when he enunciated an Emergentist view of *niyāma*. However, Jones notes that Ledi Sayadaw did not concur with this view of evolution and instead characterised *dhamma-niyāma* as the "'order of nature' as a whole, within which universal category the other four kinds of *niyāma* are particular categories of order in nature" (Jones 2012: 575). This is not what *dhamma-niyāma* means in the source texts. Rhys Davids seems to take Sayadaw's crticisms to heart and drops the discussion of *niyāma* from 1934 revised version of her book (Jones 2012: 575).

According to Pranke (2011), Ledi Sayadaw learned vipassana from "U Hpo Hlaing (1830–1883) who was notable for his *avid interest in western science and efforts to reconcile this new perspective with Abhidhamma*." (460. Emphasis added).[119] We sometimes assume that the urge to reconcile modernity and the Buddhist tradition comes solely from the West and impacts a passive Asian culture. However, Asians themselves were also modernisers and actively adopted Western perspectives and applied them to the tradition.

Having become familiar with these ideas it seemed that all that could be said about *niyāma* in modern Buddhism had been said. However, serendipitously I was reading Richard H. Jones's book *Analysis & the Fullness of Reality* (2013) on reductionism and antireductionism when I came across this passage:

> "All British emergentists accepted at least these levels: the physical, the chemical, the biological, and the psychological. In [Samuel] Alexander's more elaborate formulation, matter emerged out of space and time; life emerged out of complex configurations of matter; conscious emerged out of biological processes; and deity emerged out of consciousness (1920)." (Jones, R.H. 2013: 28)

---

[119] I'm grateful to David Chapman for this reference, via his blog post: *Theravada reinvents meditation* (7 Jul 2011). https://vividness.live/2011/07/07/theravada-reinvents-meditation/

At first glance the similarity between this view and some presentations of *niyāma* in English are striking. For Rhys Davids, the five-fold *niyāma* shows a moral order operating in the universe at different levels represented by four levels of scientific enquiry, with the addition of an overarching drive to perfection. Nārada, Ledi Sayadaw, and Sangharakshita draw out the emergent nature of this scheme by describing how phenomena at different levels are related. And finally, Sangharakshita makes the leap into treating his *niyāma* scheme as a metaphysical theory that explains causation and cosmology.

The question raised by Richard Jones is whether Caroline Rhys Davids' formulation of *niyāma* was influenced by the British Emergentists and, if so, then to what extent. Before dealing with the British Emergentists however, we need to say a word about Auguste Comte.

Comte

Auguste Comte (1798–1857) is relevant to this story because of his idea that sciences could be classified into a hierarchy. His hierarchy was anthropocentric, in that it had the study of human beings individually and collective at the top, but it is still found in popular references to science.[120] His core work was a series of books called the *Cours de Philosophie Positive*, published between 1830 and 1842. These were condensed and translated into English by Harriet Martineau and published as *The Positive Philosophy of Auguste Comte* (1853). In the *Cours* Comte was attempting a general account of human knowledge that would enable him to incorporate all branches of knowledge under one overarching scheme. It is in this work that Comte first proposes that

---

[120] See for example: https://xkcd.com/435/

the sciences can be organised based on how general they are and what level of complexity they deal with.[121]

At the base of Comte's hierarchy was mathematics, the most general and abstract form of human knowledge (1853: 25). For Comte astronomy represents the most general of the actual sciences. Next inorganic and organic phenomena, where "inorganic" corresponds to what we would call physics and chemistry, while "organic" refers to biology (cf. 1853: 27). Physiology, by which he means *human* physiology is next and then comes what he calls social physics (presaging the study of sociology).

Comte was a formative influence on J. S. Mill. After he read the *Cours*, Mill corresponded with Comte, though he later attacked Comte on various grounds (Bourdeau 2018). Mill rejected the idea that the study of the mind would be physiological in character. With the emergence of psychology as a field of study, the hierarchy of sciences shifted to include it between biology and sociology (partly in line with the individualistic attitudes of classical liberals like Mill). It was probably through George Croom Robertson that Caroline Rhys Davids because familiar with the idea of the hierarchy of sciences.

With an overview of Comte in mind, we can now turn to the British Emergentists.

The British Emergentists.

The Emergentists were a small group of British philosophers active in the late 19th and early 20th Century. They can be seen as responding to the early successes of reductionist/analytical approaches to knowledge (i.e. science) which had led many philosophers to the conclusion that an unrelenting reductionism would reveal a mechanistic world in which human beings were just one more kind of machine. The basic premise of emergentisim (aka holism or antireductionism) is that some phenomena

[121] The anthropocentric nature of this scheme is easily repudiated in the modern world, but this would distract from making the connection with Rhys Davids' thinking.

cannot be understood by reduction to lower-level causes, but only by considering a complex phenomenon as an integrated whole with its own causal efficacy. Where reductionists attribute realness only to the lowest level of causality or substance, Emergentists argued that if integrated wholes acted as irreducible effective causes, then they could also be considered real. While they accepted *substance reductionism*, the idea that everything was made of irreducible atoms, the way Emergentists treated complex objects (such as molecules) as wholes is an early form of *structure antireductionism* (R. H. Jones 2013: 27-30). Arguably, this distinction owes a good deal to Aristotle's *hylomorphism* in which he distinguishes between elements from which something is composed and the form that it takes. This combination of *substance reductionism* and *structure antireductionism* has recently re-emerged as a promising way of looking at the universe.

From the Emergentists who were active before the publication of Rhys Davids (1912), three works stand out: John Stuart Mill's *System of Logic* (1843), Alexander Bain's *Logic* (1870), and George Henry Lewes's *Problems of Life and Mind* (1875).[122] Although surveys of emergentisim (Goldstein 2014, McLaughlin 2008, and O'Connor & Wong 2015) cite these works as Emergentist, in practice they were far less committed to the idea than were the Emergentist authors of the 1920s. At best, they provided some precursory theory and inspiration to the Emergentists proper. Some of the Emergentists of the 1920s, e.g. Samuel Alexander, acknowledge no debt to the 19th Century Emergentists. Given this, at the very least we should distinguish the early *British Emergentists* (Mill, Lewes, and Bain) from the later (Alexander, Morgan, Broad, et al.). In this article, we are solely concerned with the earlier group.

Surveys I consulted also neglect to mention that Mill, Lewes, and Bain were personal friends of a similar age, who frequently met at Mill's house (Bain 1882: 65), i.e. they were not working independently but were all members of a London social clique. Bain's *Logic* (first

---

[122] McLaughlin (2008) identifies other main contributions in Samuel Alexander's *Space, Time, and Deity* (1920), Lloyd Morgan's *Emergent Evolution* (1923), and C. D. Broad's *The Mind and Its Place in Nature* (1925).

published 1870) is praised by Mill in 1872, in the preface of the 8th edition of his *A system of Logic* (see Mill 1919: vi). Mill used examples supplied by Bain (McLaughlin 2008).

John Stuart Mill (1806-1873)

J S Mill (1843) starts the ball rolling in *System of Logic* (1843), by arguing for a distinction between merely additive causes (*homopathic*) that give rise to phenomena at the same level; and combinations of causes (*heteropathic*) that in acting together cause an entirely new type of event that cannot be explained by reducing the whole to its parts.

The paradigm for the first type of causality was drawn from classical mechanics. If a stationary object is acted on by two forces exerted in a northerly (F_1) and westerly (F_2) direction, then the resultant force (F_R) will be the vector sum of the forces.[123] In other words, an object subject to the resultant force will move to the north and to the west as if first one and then the other force had been applied separately. Such forces are additive, or in Mills terms *homopathic*. The corollary is that any observed force may be resolved into orthogonal vectors, which is useful, for example, when one of the forces is gravity (acting vertically downwards).

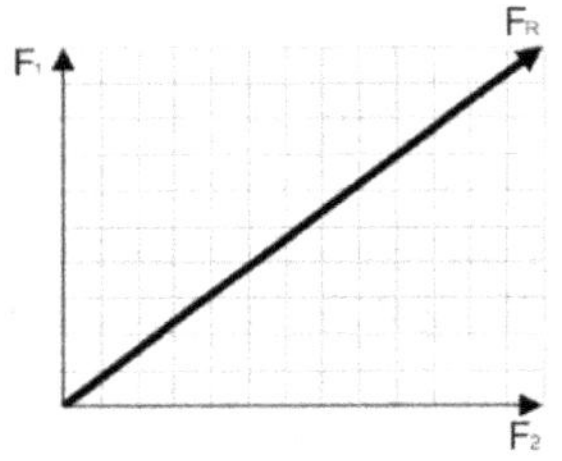

The paradigm for heteropathic causality was chemistry. At the time, it was known that matter consisted of atoms, but they were thought to be literally irreducible or atomic. J. J. Thomson discovered the electron in 1897 and Ernest Rutherford observed the first evidence for the atomic nucleus in 1911. So when the early Emergentists were writing, chemistry was not yet explicable in terms of the properties atoms (McLaughlin 2008: 55). Under these constraints, we can take the example of a water molecule, made from two hydrogen atoms combined

[123] A vector sum combines both direction and magnitude.

with an oxygen atom. The resultant molecule of water is a causal agent whose effects could not be understood in terms of the known properties of either hydrogen or oxygen atoms. In other words, the properties of water cannot be understood as the additive sum of the properties of hydrogen and oxygen. The water molecule functions as an integral whole with new properties bestowed by the structure of the molecule that are not predicted by the properties of its elements.

Mill recognised three such levels or types of causality:

> Those bodies continue, as before, to obey mechanical and chemical laws, in so far as the operation of those laws is not counteracted by the new laws which govern them as organized beings. (Mill 1876: 410)

These different types of laws correspond to what we would call physics, chemistry, and biology. This seemed a natural taxonomy at the time. Biology was distinct from chemistry because of the mysterious properties of living things that were explained in terms of a vital spark. Well into the twentieth-century some chemists supposed that a specific "chemical force" would be discovered to explain how atoms interacted. Instead, chemistry was eventually explained by a combination of the electromagnetic force and the mechanics of sub-atomic particles.

George Henry Lewes (1817-1878)

Like Mill, Lewes saw reality as being divided into distinct levels that were described by different sciences. According to Lewes

> "Among the broad distinctions of phenomena those of Physical, Chemical, and Vital [i.e. biological] must be maintained, expressing as they do the characteristic motions of propulsion, motions of combination, and motions of evolution. A chemical combination, even if finally reducible to physical laws, is markedly distinguished by *presenting new structural relations*. A still broader demarcation is given in the vital phenomenon of Evolution (characterised by

> Nutrition, Development, and Decay, through serial changes), distinguishable from the chemical combinations *out of which it emerges*. (1875: 112. Emphasis added)

Lewes is credited with the first to use the term *emergent* for this kind of causality (O'Connor & Wong 2015).

> All quantitative relations are componental; all qualitative relations elemental. The combinations of the first issue in Resultants, which may be analytically displayed; the combinations of the other *issue in Emergents*, which cannot be seen in the elements, nor deduced from them. A number is seen to be the sum of its units; a direction of movement is seen to be the line which would be occupied by the body if each of the incident forces had successively acted on it during an infinitesimal time; but a chemical or vital product is a combination of elements which cannot be seen in the elements. *It emerges from them as a new phenomenon*. (1875: 98. Emphasis added)

He also distinguished between *linear* systems, in which the trail of causality could be followed as a sequence of steps, and *non-linear* systems, in which the steps leading up to an event cannot be traced. One of the best examples of a non-linear system is weather. At any given moment, we know all of the processes that go towards creating weather, but the actual atmosphere is so complex and interactive that we cannot trace the sequence of causes that created the weather we have. Nor can we accurately predict future weather beyond a few days.

However, as McLaughlin notes, "Emergentism does not feature heavily in [Lewes] work. His primary aim is to defend British Empiricism" (2008: 31).

Alexander Bain (1818-1903)

Alexander Bain was a protégé and friend John Stuart Mill, who wrote on philosophy, logic, and psychology. In 1876, Bain founded the first psychological journal entitled *Mind*, which was edited by his protégé, George Croom Robertson (Rhys Davids psychology teacher).

Bain followed Mill in his understanding of the world being layered so that different sciences aimed to study reality at different levels. He enumerated seven levels:

> I. Logic, II. Mathematics, III. Mechanics or Mechanical Physics, IV. Molecular Physics, V. Chemistry, VI. Biology, VII. Psychology. In every one of these, there is a distinct department of phenomena; taken together, they comprehend all known phenomena, and the order indicated is the order from simple to complex, and from independent to dependent, marking the order of study and of evolution. (1870 I: 25-6)

Bain also uses chemistry as the paradigm of Emergentism, defining chemistry as "a continuation of Molecular Physics, having more especial reference to the Combinations and Decompositions, named chemical, and characterised by great accompanying *changes in properties*." (1870 I: 26. Emphasis added). He notes:

> "The mixing of materials, and the union of forces, are not the same fact.
>
> In Chemical action, thus understood, we cannot fully predict the characters of the compound from the characters of the elements. It is the speciality of the chemical combination to merge nearly all the physical properties of the substances combined, and to yield a new product, where the combining elements are not recognizable." Bain (1870 II: 40)

He also says that though Chemical Combination has been applied as a metaphor in psychology and sociology, "these, however, are mere analogies... the analogy fails in one essential circumstance, definite combinations" (1870 II: 40). Bain was not committed to Emergentism at all levels of reality.

Emergentists were responding to the idea of an ultimately mechanistic universe realised through rigorous application of reductionist analysis. They pointed out that some phenomena, especially in chemistry and biology, could not be understood (at least in the terms of the day) through reduction. In making these distinctions, they were tacitly influenced by two contemporary views. Firstly, Vitalism, the idea that some *élan vital*, life-force or living essence was what distinguished living from non-living matter. It is this "life force" that distinguishes biology from chemistry.

The scientific assault on Vitalism had begun in 1828 when German chemist, Friedrich Wöhler, reported that he had synthesised an organic compound, urea, from inorganic substrates, cyanic acid and ammonia. Since that time, Vitalism has been thoroughly discredited as a scientific theory. However, the distinction between the world of biology and psychology is still as hotly disputed now as it was in the 19th century. The mind/body problem continues to dog philosophy, psychology, and science more generally. Attempts to explain the mind in substance reductive terms have failed. And yet substance reductionism is the most accurate description of reality that we have to date. Many philosophers now acknowledge substance reductionism, but adopt a structure antireductionist or feature antireductionist approach, arguing that the properties and activities of the mind must be understood in terms of emergent properties and cannot be understood in terms of lower-level structures or features. In this view, while the brain is reducible to the fundamentals of physics, consciousness is an irreducible emergent phenomenon with distinctive properties or features. This allows philosophers to take an antiphysicalist view of consciousness without committing to substance dualism.

Another view that influenced the Emergentists was anthropomorphism. The hierarchy of levels they distinguished is not based on natural categories. They were not only influenced by Vitalism, but also by the view that evolution had produced a hierarchy of organisms that had evolved to differing degrees, with humans as the most highly evolved. This view probably derives from the Great Chain of Being. These philosophers were all atheists, who no longer saw God at the upper terminus of the Great Chain of Being, but had simply swapped God as the zenith of a hierarchy created by Him, for an *evolved* hierarchy with "Man" at the pinnacle. The transition from physics, through chemistry and biology, to psychology and sociology, is based on human notions of what makes human beings the highest form of life. With the collapse of Vitalism and with the constant extension of the properties of consciousness to other animals, this hierarchy is far less plausible now than it was in the 1870s (or in 1912). The introduction of cladistics into taxonomy has lead to the recognition that all organisms current alive are *equally* evolved. Every organism alive now is the product of four billion years of evolution.

Brian McLaughlin argued that 20th Century Emergentism did not survive the establishment of quantum mechanics, which provided the missing explanation for chemistry. However, this view has been vigorously challenged (see Goldstein 2014: 132f.). Whatever the reason, no significant works on Emergentism were published after 1925. Still, the ideas of *emergence* and *emergent properties* remained in play and are increasingly influential. The twentieth-century Emergentists, particularly Samuel Alexander, are more influential *as Emergentists* than Mill, Lewes, and Bain (O'Connor and Wong 2015). Emergent phenomena are increasingly being recognised as important. For example, they form an integral part of Constructor Theory, an attempt by David Deutch and Chiara Marletto to reformulate the laws of physics in terms of possible and impossible transformations.[124]

Caroline Rhys Davids (1857-1942)

Dr Caroline Augusta Foley Rhys Davids, along with her husband, Professor T. W. Rhys Davids (1943-1922), was at the forefront of early British efforts to rebrand Buddhism from foreign idolatry to a rational replacement for Christianity. They both wrote popular books re-

[124] See Marletto's website for an overview and a list of publications: https://www.chiaramarletto.com/

presenting Buddhism for the British public in a more digestible Modernised (or Westernised) form than it had previously taken.

The young Caroline Foley was a gifted scholar of languages, who chose to study philosophy, politics, and economics at University College London for a B.A. (1885-6). She notably won the John Stuart Mill Scholarship for Philosophy and the Joseph Hume Scholarship. Rhys Davids completed an M.A. in philosophy (1889). She was elected a fellow of the University College, London in the same year. She held academic posts at Victoria University, Manchester (1910-13) and the University of London (1918-33) (Horner 1942-3, Revell 1984, Neal 2014). Rhys Davids was awarded an honorary D.Litt degree by the Victoria University[125] in 1919, though she was still commonly referred to as *Mrs* Rhys Davids (rather than Dr.).

Although accounts of her academic work understandably emphasise her work on Pāli texts, Rhys Davids (writing as Caroline A. Foley) also made early contributions to economics, serving on the editorial board of the *Economic Journal* (1891-5); contributing articles (e.g. 1894a) including a now-classic article on economics and fashion (1893a)[126]; and translating articles on economics from German, French, and Italian for the *Economic Journal* (1892-1900), including the influential article on monetary theory by Menger (1892). She is listed in the *Biographical Dictionary of Women Economists* (Dimand et al. 2000: 129ff.). In 1896, she also published two volumes of edited lecture notes by her (then deceased) psychology tutor George Croom Robertson (Robertson 1896a, 1896b). *Buddhism: A Study of the Buddhist Norm* (Rhys Davids 1912) in which she first enunciated the concept of niyāma, is dedicated to her two university teachers G. Croom Robertson and T. W. Rhys Davids.

Rhys Davids published her first works on Buddhism before her marriage in 1894 (Foley 1893c, 1894b). With encouragement from her teacher, Professor Rhys Davids, she learned Pāli and began pioneering work on those texts that engaged her interests in psychology and feminism, i.e. the *Abhidhamma* and the *Therīgāthā*. With the help of the

[125] Now the University of Manchester.

[126] On the influence of her fashion article, see Fullbrook (1998).

modernising Burmese bhikkhu, Ledi Sayadaw (1846-1923), she quickly became the leading authority on *Abhidhamma* in the English speaking world. Rhys Davids was the Honorary Secretary of the Pali Text Society from 1907[127] and President from 1922-42. She made an inestimable contribution to the foundation of Buddhist studies in the West through her work as editor, translator, and interpreter, publishing, in addition, many works on Buddhism for a general audience.

Rhys Davids experienced what we might call a "spiritual crisis" with the death of her son, Arthur, a fighter ace who was killed in 1917 during the First World War. After this, like many others during that time, she turned to Spiritualism (with the promise of post-mortem contact with Arthur's soul) for comfort. (Revell 1984; Mackersey 2012).[128] After Thomas also died in 1922, Rhys Davids spent the last twenty years of her life seeking to extract from the Pāli texts an "original" Buddhism oriented towards finding support for her Spiritualism derived beliefs.[129] Since the opinions she espoused during this last phase of her life were heterodox, not to say unorthodox, Rhys Davids is often viewed with suspicion by modern scholars. This is a shame, as her pre-1917 work in philology, philosophy and psychology is exemplary for its time. Her later work on the Pāli texts is still important, for the methods she developed for dealing with issues of stratification and relative dating of texts within the Pāli Canon. In unpublished comments, Sangharakshita has highly praised the work of this period, arguing that it has to be taken on merit:

> "Sometimes she's very good indeed, especially her whole treatment of the idea of growth and becoming, and that what the Buddha was talking about was not just cessation, and the waning out of the unskilful, but growth and development in the skilful, in the good, right up to the point of *Nirvāṇa*,

[127] According to Horner (1942-3) she was secretary since its inception in 1881, but this is implausible.

[128] MacKersey (2012) provides a moving and insightful account of the events surrounding Arthur's death and family's reactions to it via letters from the Rhys Davids archives.

[129] For a succinct summary of her late views, see Horner (1942-3).

which was the culmination of the whole process. Thus from several points of view her work is very valuable indeed." (1973: 109)

In considering Rhys Davids as the author of a new interpretation of *niyāma*, we need to establish two propositions. Firstly, we must establish that in her interpretative works she was re-interpreting Buddhism in light of Western philosophy. Secondly, we need to establish that she was influenced by the British Emergentists.

Neal (2014) makes the case for the first of these two propositions:

"... careful reading of her introduction to [the *Dhammasaṅgaṇī* translation from 1910] reveals that Rhys Davids wove a Western interpretation of Buddhism based on comparative philosophy [and] psychology..." (22)

Similarly, in the preface of her translation of the *Abhidhammattha Saṅgaha*, Rhys Davids states that it is the first work of "Buddhist philosophy by East and West working hand-in-hand," (cited in Neal 2014: 24) and that Westerners might struggle to understand *Abhidhamma* because they (and she includes herself in this) "approach the subject wearing spectacles of our own Greek tradition..." and as Neal observes, "In other words, Rhys Davids' editorial reframing of the [*Abhidhammattha Saṅgaha*] was a self-aware, conscious process" (Neal 2014: 25).

In the memorial volume of the *Pali Text Society Journal* published after the death of Thomas, Rhys Davids reproduced his 1877 Hibbert Lecture, where for the first time he "translated *bodhi* as "Enlightenment" and explicitly compared the Buddha with the philosophers of the European Enlightenment" (McMahan 2008: 18). Judith Snodgrass (2007) concludes her summary of the contribution of the Rhys Davids to defining modern Buddhism:

"The work of the Rhys Davids undeniably took place in a colonial context and exhibits many of the key characteristics of Orientalism described by Said. Most obvious, it created an object that had much more to do with Western concerns of the time that with the lived reality of Asia." (201)

With respect specifically to *niyāma*, Jones (2012) highlights the teleological elements in Rhys Davids' interpretation:

"Rhys Davids invented her interpretation of *dhamma-niyāma* as "the effort of nature to produce a perfect type" from a need to present Buddhism in terms of evolution to a Western audience," (571).

So we can say that Rhys Davids is widely perceived as having been involved in a creative re-interpretation of Buddhism in light of Western philosophy and psychology, in which she was well versed. And this was, at least to some extent, her view of her project as well. However, I disagree with the presentation of her project as an essentially rationalist one. For example, she also says:

"But how had it been with us, if in olden time some prophet had arisen, who had seen, in a vision of universal natural law, not a philosophic theory only, nor a scientific induction, but a saving Truth, a Religion . . . . (101)"

In these words, Rhys Davids is expressing a fundamentally *religious* point of view. In *Buddhism* (1912), she expressed her belief that the universe must have a "moral order" and that it was developing towards a "perfect type". These are not rationalist ideas they are religious ideas. Most rationalists would deny that the universe has a moral order. Equally, no form of Darwinian evolution has proposed the kind of teleological interpretation adopted by Rhys Davids. In this sense, we can see her turn to Spiritualism not as fall from grace or retrogression, as is sometimes suggested, but as a natural expression of religious urges that were evident in her discussion of *niyāma* in 1912 (five year before Arthur's death). No doubt, rationalism was an aspect of her project, but the essentially irrational, religious dimension of it should not be overlooked.

Having established that her project was revisionist and, at least in some respects religious, we now need to look for connections to the British Emergentists. We have seen that the principal figures of the Emergentist movement before the publication of her 1912 book *Buddhism: a Study of the Buddhist Norm* were Mill, Lewes, and Bain. Rhys Davids, a recipient of the John Stuart Mill Scholarship, studied psychology and philosophy with George Croom Robertson, a former pupil and protégé of Alexander Bain. Her account of her former teacher is both effusive when considering his methods and wry on the subject of his personality (Foley: 1893b).[130] Rhys Davids edited two volumes of Robertson's lecture notes into books after he died (Robertson 1896a, 1896b). In the first of these volumes, the one on psychology Robertson says of Bain:

> Professor Bain has been the most important contributor to psychology in England in this century. His pre-eminence extends over the whole field of psychology as distinct from philosophy (1896a: 117-118).

Robertson was, however, critical of Bain's failure to consider the individual in their social context, a feature of the early Emergentists thinking. As George Lewes (1875) says, "All the attempts to explain Mind without taking the social factors into account have been signal failures."

Bain, as we have seen, was one of the central figures of British Emergentism as well as a personal friend of both Mill and Lewes. Robertson provides us with a potential link between the Emergentists and Rhys Davids. Bain's book *Mental Science* (1868) was required reading for Robertson's curriculum, though it does not contain any obvious reference to Emergentism, despite frequently discussing J. S. Mill. In the volume of Robertson's lecture notes on psychology edited by Rhys Davids (Robertson 1896a), we do find an echo of Emergentism

[130] According to one source, it was Robertson who sent the undergraduate Caroline Foley to see her future husband, Professor T W Rhys Davids, because of her interest in Indian philosophy (Revell 1984: 14).

in the first two lectures. In trying to describe how one might get knowledge of the mind in his first lecture, Robertson describes the sciences in terms of decreasing generality and increasing speciality: Mathematics, Physics, Chemistry, Biology, Psychology, and Sociology (Robertson 1896a: 4-5, 6). But the relations between these sciences are not discussed, instead, he continues trying to define the subject of psychology. Robertson appears to adopt a different stance to the Emergentists:

> "We are familiar with the fact that all changes of bodies or media are ultimately reducible to modes of motion, as e.g. sound, light, heat; and again in chemistry, where a chemical reaction is only a rearrangement of atoms in space, i.e. motion. ... We can never make a physical disturbance *pass into* a psychical disturbance. This implies [45] the important fact that there is no accounting for mind in terms of matter, though we *may* explain matter in terms of mind. But this is metaphysical ground." (45-6)

Still, it is very likely that in the course of her study of philosophy and psychology, Rhys Davids became acquainted with the work of John Stuart Mill and probably Bain. Robertson frequently cites the works of Bain, and so it also seems likely that as a conscientious student, Rhys Davids would have read some of these. It is thus likely, though of course not definite, that when she listed the phases of the moral order she perceived in *niyāma*, that she had Emergentism in mind.

Comte's Hierarchy	Croom's Hierarchy	Rhys David's Hierarchy
		Order of the norm
Social physics (mental)	Sociology	
Physiology (organic)	Psychology	Order of the mind
Chemistry (inorganic)	Biology	Physical organic order
Physics	Chemistry	Physical inorganic order
Astronomy	Physics	
Maths	Mathematics	
		Order of act-and-result

The Rhys David's scheme cannot correspond completely to the Comtean scheme since she has to squeeze in *karma* and *dhamma*. Karma she relegates to the lowest level (whereas Sangharakshita promotes it to the second-highest position), and dharma she recasts as the "norm" rather than "nature". Starting with the idea that a buddha's life story follows a template, Rhys Davids come up with the *telos* that nature "wants" to produce a perfect type, i.e. a buddha. As I noted above, this is a religious, teleological outlook rather than a rationalist one.

Rhys David's use of "organic" and "inorganic" divisions of physical phenomena is reminiscent of Comte's hierarchy of sciences (1853: 26-33). However, this is the closest I have been able to come in finding a link between them.

Thus, we can say that the first of our two propositions is firmly supported by direct evidence that Rhys Davids was well versed in the philosophy of the day is clear from her studies, her receipt of the John Stuart Mill Scholarship at university, and her editorship of Robertson's lecture notes. Rhys Davids own works and in the interpretations of those works by many scholars suggest that she was, along with her husband, re-interpreting Buddhism in light of Western philosophy.

The second of our propositions, that she was influenced by the British Emergentists is not supported directly, but there is considerable circumstantial evidence of a potential influence on Rhys Davids.

Conclusions

This study aimed to determine whether or not Caroline Rhys Davids had the means, motive, and opportunity to borrow from the British Emergentists for her *niyāma* scheme. We have seen that Rhys Davids is widely considered to have been involved in reinterpreting Buddhism in light of Western philosophy and psychology. She was a gifted student and well versed in philosophy both European and Indian.

The *niyāma* scheme found in Rhys Davids (1912) is a creative re-interpretation of the scheme found in Buddhaghosa's commentarial texts. The approaches of Buddhaghosa and Rhys David to *niyāma*, though related, were divergent. Both were interested in the idea of a moral universe, what we might nowadays call a Just-World Hypothesis, expressed in the form of the Buddhist doctrine of karma. The impersonal, almost mechanistic, nature of the karma doctrine seemed to appeal to her. To this, Rhys Davids, initially at least, added the idea of evolution toward a "perfect type" in the form of a Buddha. However, she also clashed with Ledi Sayadaw over this teleological interpretation and appears to have stepped back from it. That said the idea of evolution and, as she called it "growth" (Horner 1942-3: 172), continued to be important to Rhys Davids' interpretation of Buddhism, where it is juxtaposed and contrasted with the idea of *nirvāṇa* as "extinction".

Rhys Davids has a personal connection with the British Emergentists, via her tutor George Croom Robertson, though Robertson himself seems not to have followed Bain in his Emergentist views. I have uncovered no evidence that Robertson actively rejected Emergentism and there are repeated complimentary references to Bain's contributions to psychology in the lecture notes (1896a, 1896b) that Rhys Davids edited after Robertson died. On this basis, we can plausibly speculate that Rhys Davids read Bain's principal works and probably those of John Stuart Mill.

Rhys Davids was certainly in the right time and place, the right academic milieu, to be exposed to the ideas of the Emergentists. Her education must surely have included some or all of their work. We know that she was a creative thinker and actively involved in re-interpreting Buddhism in ways that she hoped would be appreciated by Europeans. And we have the fact that her *niyāma* scheme resembles similar schemes discussed by the Emergentists. However, Rhys Davids diverged from the Emergentists by giving the scheme a religious tone through the ideas of universal moral order and evolution toward a perfect type. The connection with the British Emergentists seems plausible enough and we may that it also seems likely.

☸

Dhammaniyāmata and idappaccayatā

In this essay, I explore the term *dhamma-niyāmatā* as it is used in the Paccaya Sutta (SN 12:20), and also make some notes about the term *idappacayatā*. This will involve comparing several versions of the text: the Pāli sutta and its counterparts in Chinese and Sanskri versions of the *Samyuktāgama* (SĀ 296). A *Samyuktāgama* manuscript was translated into Chinese by Guṇabhadra (求那跋陀羅) in the Liu Song 劉宋 period (435–443 CE). However, there is also a Sanskrit text from a cache found at Turfan. It was copied much later, probably around the 13th Century. We begin with the Pāli and the passage of interest is:

> Whether anyone is awakened or not, the principle remains: the fact of mental events being conditioned, the fixed course of mental phenomena, and specific conditionality [of mental phenomena].[131]

More literally the first phrase is "arising of a *tathāgata* or non-arising of a *tathāgata*". *Tathāgata* is how the Buddha referred to himself and it generally means someone who has realised *nirvāṇa* or attained awakening. Tradition usually tells us that *tathāgata* means "thus gone" but *-gata* as a the second member of a compound takes the sense of "in" or "being in". So for example, *citragata* does not mean "gone to the picture", it means "in the picture". So we expect *tathāgata* to mean "in that state".

"The principle remains" translates *ṭhitāva sā dhātu*. Here, *thitāva* resolves to *ṭhitā eva*. *Ṭhita* (Skt *sthita*) is the past participle of the verb *tiṭṭhati* (Skt *tiṣṭhati* from the root √*sthā* "to stand, remain"). A *ṭhita* is something lasting or enduring. The long final *ā* tells us that *ṭhita* is being used as an adjective of *dhātu*, a feminine noun. *Dhātu* can have a range of meanings including "element; natural condition, property; factor, item, principle." If we take *ṭhitā dhātu* as a unit, then we expect meanings such as "abiding principle", "established property", or

---

131 *uppādā vā tathāgatānaṃ anuppādā vā tathāgatānaṃ, ṭhitāva sā dhātu dhammaṭṭhitatā dhammaniyāmatā idappaccayatā.* (SN II.25)

"enduring natural condition". In other words, it is a state of affairs that remains in play. The particle *eva* emphasises the endurance of the principle.

"The fact of mental events being conditioned" translates *dhammaṭṭhitatā. Ṭhitatā* is an abstract noun from the same past participle (*ṭhita*). The *Pali Text Society Dictionary* suggests it means "the fact of standing or being founded on". In other words, the connotation is different than for *ṭhita*. The word is mainly used in precisely this context as a quality of *dhammas*. As we know, conditioned (*saṅkhata*) dhammas arise (*samuppāda*) in dependence on a condition (*paccaya*). Dependence (literally "hanging down from") is an inversion of the cognitive metaphor involved in the Pāli word *paṭicca* (Skt *pratītya*), which is from the root *prati√i* and means "going back to, returning". This also gives us the title of the sutta, *paccaya* (Skt. *pratyaya*). A dhamma (literally "support") springs-up (*samuppāda*) when the condition (*paccaya*) that supports it (from below) is in place. I take *dhamma-ṭṭhitatā* to be a reference to the principle of conditionality. And that we can take it to mean that the principle of conditionality is an abiding principle (*ṭhitā dhātu*).

As explained elsewhere in the book, *niyāma* means "a fixed course; constrained; inevitably". In the context of *dhamma-niyāmatā* "the fact of the fixed course of *dhammas*", this means that *dhammas* don't get a choice. When the conditions are in place, *dhammas* must arise; when the conditions are absent *dhammas* must either not arise or having arisen they must cease. Buddhaghosa relates this to the inevitability and inescapability of the ripening karma (c.f. Attwood 2014). So again this is a reference to the principle of conditionality.

Finally, the abiding principle is also *idappaccayatā* (Skt. *idampratyayatā*). The etymology is fairly obvious (more so in Sanskrit) but difficult to articulate in English. The whole thing is an abstract noun, so refers to an abstraction from the idea of *idaṃ pratyaya* "this condition" or "whose condition is this". However we get there, the word refers to the specificity of the conditions: specific conditions give rise to specific results. In other words, there is an order to how dependent arising functions: it has to function and it has to function in a particular way that relates consequence to action: A good intention (*kusalā cetanā*) gives rise to a good result (*kusala phala*); if there is a good result we can infer a good intention as the condition. We can see, therefore, that *idappaccayatā* is the same quality as Buddhaghosa's *bījaniyāma* (like for like), perhaps combined with *utuniyāma* (timeliness).

We might call this a law of nature. A law of nature is always applicable, always gives the same result given the same causes. It is a *ṭhitā dhātu* or a *niyāma*. With this in mind, let us now turn to the Chiense version of the *Pratyaya Sūtra.*

The Chinese. SĀ 296

The Samyuktāgama parallel with Choong Mun-keat's translation is

> 若佛出世，若未出世，此法常住，法住法界 (T2.84.b17-18)

> "Whether a Buddha arises in the world, or not, this is the unchangeable nature of dharma, the status of dharma, the element of dharma." (Choong 2010: 45)[132]

Choong (1999: 19) leads us to believe that certain Pāli and Middle Chinese terms are equivalents, i.e.

dhammaṭṭhitatā = *fǎ zhù* 法住
dhammaniyāmatā = *fǎ dìng* 法定
idappaccayatā = *fǎ jiè* 法界

This cannot be right. What we have in the Chinese *Pratyaya Sūtra* is *fǎ cháng zhù* 法常住, *fǎ zhù* 法住, *fǎ jiè* 法界. Under 法常住, the *Digital Dictionary of Buddhism* suggests "the Dharma that is eternally abiding". But I think the pronoun *cǐ* 此 in the text implies *dharmāḥ* in

---

[132] In the *Sutta Central* metadata this translation is credited as "originally published in" Choong (1999) but it is not translated in that book as far as I can tell. Rather, it is translated in Choong (2010).

the plural, meaning mental phenomena rather than the *Dharma* (singular). This fits with my reading of the Pāli compounds. So a translation like "*dharmas* abide eternally" is more likely, though this is quite problematic from a Theravāda point of view (I'll return to this point at the end of this section).

Note that the text has taken a shortcut. There is no equivalent to *ṭhitāva sā dhātu* "the principle remains". Although we do have the characters we need for it, i.e. *zhù jiè* 住界 "abiding principle".

The problem here is that *fǎ cháng zhù* 法常住 "dharmas eternally remain" is followed by more or less the same word, i.e. *fǎ zhù* 法住 "*dharmas* remain". We are expecting to find *fǎ dìng* 法定, the equivalent of *dhammaniyāmatā*. In other words, this appears to be a scribal error with repetition/substitution of 住 for 定. Such errors are very common in copied manuscripts.

Choong glosses over (and thus hides) the repetition by choosing different translations for the two phrases, viz. "the unchangeable nature of dharma" and "the status of dharma". Here "nature" and "status" both translate *zhù* 住 "stay behind, remain; pause, halt". *Zhù* 住 is commonly used to translate words deriving from Sanskrit √*sthā* "abide, stand, remain" since the semantic fields substantially overlap. It is also used to translate the verb *viharati* "dwelling, abiding".

Moreover, the characters *fǎ zhù* 法界 do not translate *idappaccayatā* but rather usually translate *dharmadhātu*, i.e. "the realm of *dharmas* qua experience" or the "experiential realm" rather than the later idea of a realm of the *Dharma*). A modern translation of *idappaccayatā* is *cǐ yuán xìng* 此缘性 but this is no help to us here precisely because it is modern and not found in the *Āgama* texts. And the reason for this took some time to appreciate.

It turns out that in the whole *Saṃyutta Nikāya* the word *idappaccayatā* only occurs here in the *Paccaya Sutta*, so there is no easy way to find out if Guṇabhadra used it in contexts other than the *Samyukatāgama*. This word is very uncommon. Across all the *Nikāyas* it only occurs one other time, in the *Ariyapariyesanā Sutta* (MN 26), and there only once. The Chinese version of MN 26, i.e. MĀ 204 omits the passage that includes the word *idappaccayatā*. The story of Brahmā's request to teach (Section 20 of MN 26) is recounted in (1st) *Ekottarikāgama* (19.1) but does not use this word. *Ekottarikāgama* 24.5 recounts part of the story but also misses out the passage of interest. So there appears to be no Chinese *Āgama* text that uses this expression.

We do find the expression in *Dàzhìdù lùn*《大智度論》 (T. 1509) a voluminous commentary on the *Large Prajñāpāramitā Sutra*, where our passage of interest is cited.

> Whether there is a Buddha or there is no Buddha, this causality (*idaṃpratyayatā*), this nature of things (*dharmatā*), is always present in the world." (Ani Migme's translation of Lamotte's French translation)[133]

However, here 因緣 seems to correspond, not to *idaṃpratyaya*, but to another common compound, *hetu-pratyaya* "causes and conditions". The character *yīn* 因 means "cause" and routinely translates *hetu* in contrast to *yuán* 緣 which routinely translates *pratyaya* "condition". The combination *fǎ xiāng* 法相 does, at least, correspond to *dharmatā*, but I think Lamotte has fudged the translation of *yīn yuán* 因緣 because he was familiar with the *Paccaya Sutta*. With hindsight, the expression *idaṃpratyayatā* is not used in SĀ 296.

Sarvāstivāda?

Earlier, I noted an anomaly in the Chinese translation *fǎ cháng zhù* 法常住 "dharmas abide eternally". The *Saṃyuktāgama* manuscript translated into Chinese is thought to have belonged to a Sarvāstivāda sect. This phrase—*fǎ cháng zhù* 法常住—may betray a Sarvāstivāda point of view.

David Bastow (1995) outlined why the Sarvāstivādins concluded that dharmas must be eternal ("always existent", i.e. *sarva-asti*). They

[133] The Chinese reads: 有佛無佛，是因緣法相續常在世間 (T. 1509; 25.253c.1-2)

began by taking the formula of dependent arising seriously. That formula is:

> When this is present, that exists,
> With the arising of this, that arises.
> When this is absent, that does not exist,
> When this ceases, then than ceases.[134]

Let us suppose that a *citta* or *dharma* characterised by greed (*lobha*) arises and then ceases. If we are to make progress as Buddhists, we have to know that we just experienced a *lobha-dharma.* This is in order that we can avoid repeating the mistake. To know this, the greed *citta* itself must be a condition for such knowledge. According to the formula: that (result) arises only when this (condition) is present. Therefore, the *lobha-dharma must still be present.* If this relation holds, then the logical outcome is that dharmas must always be present, i.e. they must always exist: *sarva-asti.* This is where the logic of the formula takes us and is by no means illogical or stupid. And this was the dominant Buddhist view in the northwest of Greater India for some centuries.

Of course, this eternality is problematic, but the Sarvāstivādins got around it by positing that dharmas are always present but only *active* in the present. This was their metaphysical manoeuvre. All Buddhists ended up having metaphysical manoeuvres to try to link consequences to actions over time (this is one of the main topics of my book on karma and rebirth). The *sarva-asti* manoeuvre is quite metaphysically conservative compared to what made it through into the modern forms of Buddhism. Buddhists tended to proliferate supernatural entities and processes to make karma work, e.g. *bhavaṅgacitta* or *ālayavijñāna.*

---

134 In the less familiar Sanskrit form that Sarvastivādins used: *Yaduta asmin satīdaṃ bhavaty asyotpadād idam utpadyate / Yaduta asmin asatīdaṃ na bhavaty asya nirodhād idaṃ nirudhyate.*

With this digression complete. we can now turn to the Sanskrit manuscript of the *Pratyaya Sūtra*, which is the latest of all our sources but may be of some use.

Pratyaya Sūtra

The *sūtra* is part of a Sanskrit *Nidānasaṃyukta* manuscript found at Turfan and edited by Chandrabhāl Tripāṭhī. It was probably copied in the thirthteenth or fourteenth century and we know very little about the provenance of it. This gives us a third version of the passage:

> *ity utpādād vā tathāgatānām anutpādād vā sthitā eveyaṃ dharmatā dharmasthitaye dhātuḥ* (Sutra 14, line 5)
>
> Thus, whether or not a tathāgatā arises, this principle remains: naturalness and the stability of dharmas.
>
> Pāli: *uppādā vā tathāgatānaṃ anuppādā vā tathāgatānaṃ, ṭhitāva sā dhātu dhammaṭṭhitatā dhammaniyāmatā idappaccayatā.* (SN II.25)

It appears to me that the Sanskrit text has become garbled. The word order has changed, partially obscuring the relation between *sthitā* and *dhātuḥ*. And we are lacking any equivalent of *idappaccayatā*.

The word *dharmatā* appears to be out of place. We are expecting to see *dharmaniyāmatā*. Meanwhile, *dharmasthitaye* has a case ending which is unexpected, since we expect to see a nominative singular. Given that the word is a feminine noun in *-ā* we don't expect to see *-aye* at all. According to Edgerton's *Buddhist Hybrid Sanskrit Grammar* (1953: 63), it does occur as a case ending for *-ā* in the *Mahāvastu*, but it is used obliquely, i.e. for all the cases from instrumental to locative and not for the nominative case that we expect (1953: 61). It is likely that *-āye* was intended, since this is more common, but again, this is the oblique case ending and it cannot be correct.

If I take the Pāli text of the second part of the passage and render it directly into Classical Sanskrit and Middle Chinese, it looks like this (followed by the actual texts for comparison):

Pāli: *ṭhitāva sā dhātu dhammaṭṭhitatā dhammaniyāmatā idappaccayatā*
Skt: *sthitaiva tāḥ dhātu dharmasthitatā dharmaniyāmatā idaṃpratyayatā*
Ch: 住即界法住法定 XXX[135]

Turfan: *sthitā eveyaṃ dharmatā dharmasthitaye dhātuḥ*
SĀ 296: ... 此法常住，法住法界.

There was nothing very difficult or complicated about either of these translations except the lack of a Chinese translation for *idappaccayatā*. The words in the Turfan ms. seem to have gotten jumbled up and fragmented so they no longer make sense. Something similar has happened to the Chinese text.

Second Phrase

If we read a little further on in the Chinese text we find a similar phrase which uses some of the same terminology (and the Pāli version once again uses the word *idappaccayatā*). Starting with the Chinese text and Choong's translation:

> 此等諸法，法住、法空、法如、法爾，法不離如，法不異如，審諦真實、不顛倒 (T 2.82.b22-4)

> All these dharmas are the status of dharma, the standing of dharma, the suchness of dharma; the dharma neither departs from things-as-they-are, nor differs from things-as-they-are; it is truth, reality, without distortion. (Choong 2010: 45-6)

---

135 XXX: stands for the missing Chinese equivalent of the word *idappaccayatā*.

Choong's note (2010: 45) reads:

> 法定 The unchangeable nature of dharma. Original Taishō text has 法空, but according to CSA[136], it should be 法定 (vol.2, p.36) (2010: 45).

In other words, the problem here is that *fă kōng* 法空 (*dharma-śūnyatā*) should be *fă dìng* 法定 (*dharma-niyāmatā*). This is consistent with the Sanskrit text. Note that the opening block of text *cǐ děng zhū fǎ* 此等諸法 is literally "these 此 many kinds 等諸 of dharmas 法", hence Choong's translation, "all these dharmas".

The Turfan Sanskrit text counterpart reads:

> *iti yātra dharmatā dharmasthititā dharmaniyāmatā dharmayathātathā avitathatā ananyathā bhūtaṃ satyatā tattvatā yāthātathā aviparītatā aviparyastatā* (14.6)

Here, *yātra* is not to be confused with the locative adverbial pronoun *yatra* "where". It must either be a mistake for *yatra* or the result of sandhi from *yā atra* "which here", where *yā* is the Prakrit relative pronoun in the feminine nominative singular. The Classical Sanskrit is *yāḥ* which would be *yā* when followed by a vowel, but would not undergo further sandhi, i.e. *yāḥ atra* > *yā atra*. The Pāli text has *yā tatra*, which appears to confirm the *yā atra* reading since *atra* and *tatra* mean much the same thing. However, overall, the Pāli has a very different vocabulary at this point.

> Thus, monks, that which is actual, not unactual, not otherwise—this is called dependent arising.[137]

---

[136] CSA = Yin (1983).

[137] *Iti kho, bhikkhave, yā tatra tathatā avitathatā anaññathatā idappaccayatā—ayaṃ vuccati, bhikkhave, paṭicca-samuppādo.*

As Bodhi (2000: 742 n.54) elsewhere notes in relation to SN 56:20, the Four Noble Truths are said to be *tatha*, *avitatha*, and *anaññatha* or in his translation "actual, unerring, and not otherwise". Buddhaghosa's commentary on SN 12:20 in the *Sāratthappakāsinī* (or *Saṃuyttanikāya Aṭṭhakathā*) gives these terms a very specific meaning: *tathatā* refers to phenomena arising when conditions are present; *avitathatā* refers to this being a non-repeating process (one set of conditions gives rise to one phenomenon), and *anaññathatā* means that each set of conditions gives rise to a phenomenon that is specific to those conditions, i.e. *anaññatha* is synonymous with *idappaccayatā*. Although Bodhi links this commentarial gloss with SN 56:20, the commentary he is translating is not the one that comes up when I look at the commentary on this text. Unfortunately, Bodhi does not say what he is translating.

Note that once again neither the Chinese nor the Sanskrit has an equivalent of *idappaccayatā*. It's not clear why they have a completely different pericope at this point. This goes beyond a simple translation issue. The text appears to have been constructed with a different pericope at this point.

Conclusion

I started off exploring the meaning of *dhamma-niyāmatā* in a *sutta* with a view to better understanding Buddhaghosa's later use of the term *niyāma* "fixed course, constraint". This quality of *dhamma-niyāmatā* is said to be an abiding principle (*ṭhitā dhātu*). It seems that it refers to the conditionality of *dhammas* qua phenomena. And thus is it not related to the way that Buddhaghosa uses the term *dhammaniyāma* to describe the miracles that accompany the milestones in the career of a *buddha*. This distinctoin is quite important for the concept of *niyāma* in Buddhism.

We have to be careful when thinking about phenomena in early Buddhism lest we inadvertently transpose a modern understanding of the concept or the terms we use. Early Buddhists seem to make a distinction between mental and physical phenomena. It seems quite likely to me that they considered physical objects to be independent of their minds, but understood that phenomena associated with such objects (i.e. how such objects appear to the mind) as like mental phenomena. But the insight is connected in their case to meditative experience in which sensory and cognitive experience cease without the loss of consciousness, what is sometimes referred to as contentless awareness. Buddhists were not Idealists in the classical sense, but they might have had some sympathies with Kant's Transcendental Idealism had they come across it.

As I understand early Buddhists, they were making an epistemic argument about the conditions under which we experience phenomena. And they were not making a metaphysical argument about the nature of objects that we experience through phenomena. Indeed, the cessation of experience in meditation eclipsed any and all metaphysical speculation in importance. This is not the same as saying that early Buddhists did not have metaphysics or that their epistemic conclusions did not have metaphysical implications. Rather, they simply never systematically developed metaphysics as a branch of philosophy. Phenomena and the nature of experience were the focus.

I argued that *dhammaṭṭhitatā* is a reference to the fact of conditionality, i.e. phenomena arising when the condition is present. Early Buddhists considered this to be an enduring law of nature, And I argued that the term *dhammaniyāmatā* is a synonym with only a slightly different connotation. That all *dhammas* (qua mental event) have a fixed course (*niyāmatā*) is a reference to the inevitability of a phenomenon arising when the condition for it is present, and the ceasing or non-arising when the condition is absent. This suggests that *dhamma-niyāmatā* in the suttas is more like Buddhaghosa's *kamma-niyāma*.

The original phrase in the *sutta* was probably: *ṭhitāva sā dhātu dhammaṭṭhitatā dhammaniyāmatā* "this fact remains: the fact of mental events being conditioned, the constraints on mental events". And since the text refers to only one fact (*sā dhātu*), we have to read *dhamma-ṭṭhitatā* and *dhamma-niyāmatā* as being synonyms, not two different terms. Contrarily, we have to read *dhamma* here as *dhammā* (plural) and as being related to phenomena qua how things appear to us, not the existence of things or the nature of their existence.

It seems that *idappaccayatā* only occurs in Theravāda texts and may be a late insertion. I could find no early Buddhist texts in other languages that contain this word, even when there are translations of texts or passages that seem to be direct parallels. There seems to be no entry in the Gāndhārī dictionary that corresponds to this word.

We also see how errors build-up to render a text confusing or even meaningless and how Chinese texts of this era read in isolation are often misleading.

☸

Bibliography

All Pāli texts are from the *Chaṭṭha Saṅgāyana Tipiṭaka*, 4th ed. published by the Vipassana Research Institute. This is based on the *Burmese Sixth Council* edition of the Tipiṭaka produced between 1954 and 1956.

Alexander, Samuel. (1920). *Space, Time, and Deity: The Gifford Lectures, 1916-1918*, Vol. 2. London: Macmillan.

Ali, S. M. and Zimmer, R. M. (1998). Emergence: A Review of the Foundations. *Systems Research and Information science*, 8, 1-24.

Almond, Philip C. (1988). The British Discovery of Buddhism. Cambridge University Press.Aussant, Emilie (2015). Vyākaraṇic Texts and Śāstric Discourse. *Journal of Value Inquiry*, Springer Verlag, 49 (4): 551-566. https://halshs.archives-ouvertes.fr/halshs-01367315/document

Attwood, Jayarava. (2012). Possible Iranian Origins for Sākyas and Aspects of Buddhism. Journal of the Oxford Centre for Buddhist Studies, 3, 47-69. http://www.ocbs.org/ojs/index.php/jocbs/article/view/26

——. (2014). "Escaping the Inescapable: Changes in Buddhist Karma." *Journal of Buddhist Ethics*, 21, 503-535. http://blogs.dickinson.edu/buddhistethics/2014/06/04/changes-in-buddhist-karma

——. (2017). "Form is (Not) Emptiness: The Enigma at the Heart of the Heart Sutra." *Journal of the Oxford Centre for Buddhist Studies*, 13, 52–80.

——. (2018a). "Defining Vedanā: Through the Looking Glass". *Contemporary Buddhism*, 18(3), 31-46. https://doi.org/10.1080/14639947.2018.1450959

——. (2018b). *Karma and Rebirth Reconsidered: An Inquiry into the Buddhist Myths of a Just World and an Afterlife*. Visible Mantra Press.

Bain, Alexander. (1882). *John Stuart Mill: A Criticism with Personal Recollections*. Longmans, Green / Thoemmes.

Bain, Alexander. (1887). *Logic. Vol II*. Rev ed. Appleton. First published 1870. https://archive.org/stream/logic00baingoog#page/n6/mode/2up

Bastow, David. (1995). The First Argument for Sarvāstivāda. *Asian Philosophy* 5(2), 109-125. Online: http://buddhism.lib.ntu.edu.tw/FULLTEXT/JR-ADM/bastow.htm

Bode, M. (1911). "Thomas William Rhys Davids; Caroline Augusta Foley Rhys Davids; The Work of Prof. and Mrs. Rhys Davids in Pāli Literature." *The Buddhist Review*, 3.2, 81-86.

Bodhi. (1993) *A Comprehensive Manual of Abhidhamma: The Abhidhammattha Sangaha of Ācariya Anuruddha*. Kandy, Sri Lanka, Buddhist Publication Society.

——. (2000). *The Connected Discourses of the Buddha: A Translation of the Saṃyutta Nikāya*. Boston: Wisdom.

Bourdeau, Michel. (2018). "Auguste Comte." In *The Stanford Encyclopedia of Philosophy* (Summer 2018 Edition), Edward N. Zalta (ed.). https://plato.stanford.edu/archives/sum2018/entries/comte/

Cappeller, Carl. (1891). *Sanskrit-English Dictionary*, Strassburg.

Chaṭṭha Saṅgāyana Tipiṭaka [Version 4]. Vipassana Research Institute. (CST)

Choong Mun-keat. (1999). *The Notion of Emptiness in Early Buddhism*. 2nd. Ed. Motilal Banarsidass.

——. (2010). *Annotated Translation of Sutras from the Chinese Samyuktāgama relevant to the Early Buddhist Teachings on Emptiness and the Middle Way*. 2nd rev. Ed. Thailand: International Buddhist College.

Crosby, Kate. (2008). Kamma, Social Collapse or Geophysics? Interpretations of Suffering among Sri Lankan Buddhists in the Immediate Aftermath of the 2004 Tsunami. *Contemporary Buddhism, 9*: 53–76.

Comte, Auguste. (1853) *The positive philosophy of Auguste Comte*. Translated and condensed by Harriet Martineau. London: John Chapman.

Dhīvan. (2009). *Sangharakshita, the Five Niyamas and the Problem of Karma*. Unpublished Essay

——. (2010) 'The Need for Doctrine: the Five Nīyamas and Western Buddhism.' (forthcoming)

—— (2013). 'The 'Five Niyamas' and Natural Order.' [Blog Post] 5 June 2013. http://dhivanthomasjones.wordpress.com/2013/06/05/the-five-niyamas-and-natural-order/

Dimand, R.W., Dimand, M. A., and Forget, E. L. (2000). *Biographical Dictionary of Women Economists*. Edward Elgar.

Edgerton, Franklin. (1953). *Buddhist Hybrid Sanskrit Dictionary*, New Haven: Yale University Press.

Foley, Caroline A. (1893a) Fashion. *The Economic Journal*. 458.

—— (1893b). George Croom Robertson as a Teacher. *Mind 2* (6): 275-280. http://www.jstor.org/stable/2247967

—— (1893c). The Women Leaders Of The Buddhist Reformation, As Illustrated By Dhammapala's Commentary On The Theri-Gatha, in *Transactions of the Ninth International Congress of Orientalists*. Vol. 1 (Indian and Aryan Sections). Ed. Morgan, E. Delmar. Committee of the Congress. 344-361.

—— (1894a). Royal Commission on Labour. The Employment of Women. *The Economic Journal 4* (13): 185-191. DOI: 10.2307/2955893. http://www.jstor.org/stable/2955893

—— (1894b). The Vedalla Sutta, as Illustrating the Psychological Basis of Buddhist Ethics. *The Journal of the Royal Asiatic Society of Great Britain and Ireland*. Apr., 1894: 321-333.

Fullbrook, Edward. (1998). Caroline Foley and the Theory of Intersubjective Demand, *Journal of Economic Issues, 709, 709–10*.

Gethin, Rupert. (2004). 'He Who Sees Dhamma Sees Dhammas: Dhamma in Early Buddhism.' *Journal of Indian Philosophy*, 32: 513–542.

Goldstein, Jeffery A. (2014). Introduction: Emergence, Complexity, Aggregation, and Transformation. *E:CO* 16(1):131-168 [introduces the reprint of Russell et al. 1926]

Havens, Teresina Rowell. (1964). Mrs. Rhys Davids' Dialogue with Psychology (1893-1924). Philosophy East and West, 14 (1), 51-58. DOI: 10.2307/1396754. Stable URL: http://www.jstor.org/stable/1396754

Horner, I. (1942-3). Caroline Rhys Davids. , 41, 172-3.

Jones, Dhivan Thomas. (2012). The Five Niyāmas as Laws of Nature: an Assessment of Modern Western Interpretations of Theravāda Buddhist Doctrine. *Journal of Buddhist Ethics*, 19. 545-582. http://blogs.dickinson.edu/buddhistethics/

—— (2013). The 'Five Niyamas' and Natural Order. *Dhivan Thomas Jones News, Views and Thoughts [blog]*. June 5, 2013. https://dhivanthomasjones.wordpress.com/2013/06/05/the-five-niyamas-and-natural-order/

Jones, Richard H. (2013). *Analysis & the Fullness of Reality: An Introduction to Reductionism & Emergence*. Jackson Square Books.

Joshi, S.D. & Roodbergen, J. (Ed. Tr) *Patanjali's Vyakarana-Mahabhashya*. Paspasha-Ahnika. Poona, 1986. Online: *scribd.com*

Kahrs, Eivind. (1998). *Indian Semantic Analysis: The Nirvacana Tradition*. Cambridge University Press.

Kielhorn, F. (Ed). *The Vyākarṇa-mahābhāṣya of Patañjali*. 3rd Ed. rev. by K. V. Abhyankar. Vol 1. 1962.

Katre, S.M. (1987). *Aṣṭādhyāyī of Pāṇini*, University of Texas Press.

Ledi Sayadaw. (1978). 'The Niyama-Dipani: The Manual of Cosmic Order,' in *The Manuals of Buddhism*, trans. Barua, B.M, Rhys Davids, C.A.F., & Nyana. Bangkok: Mahamakut Press (orig. publ. 1965). Online: www.dhammaweb.net/html/view.php?id=5 [includes Sayadaw's correspondence with Rhys Davids showing how her interpretation is dependent on his]

Lewes, George Henry. 1875. *Problems of Life and Mind. Vol.2.* London: Kegan Paul, Trench, Turber. https://archive.org/details/problemsoflifemi01leweiala

MacDonnell, A.A. (1893). *A Sanskrit-English Dictionary*. London: Longmans.

MacKersey, Ian. (2012). *No Empty Chairs: The Short and Heroic Lives of the Young Aviators Who Fought and Died in the First World War*. London: Weidenfeld & Nicolson.

Mahony. William K. (1997). *The Artful Universe: An Introduction to the Vedic Religious Imagination*. State University of New York Press.

Magnus, Margaret. (1999).*Gods of the Word: Archetypes in the Consonants.* Thomas Jefferson University Press.

McDermott, J. P. (1989) 12(1) The Kathāvatthu Niyāma Debates. *Journal of the International Association of Buddhist Studies*. 139-146.

McLaughlin, Brian P. (2008) The Rise and Fall of British Emergentism, in *Emergence*. MIT Press.

McMahan, David L. (2008). *The Making of Buddhist Modernism*. Oxford University Press.

Menger, Carl. 1892. On the Origin of Money. [Trans. Caroline A. Foley] *Economics Journal*, 92: 239-55.

Mill, John Stuart. (1868). *A system of logic, ratiocinative and inductive; being a connected view of the principles of evidence and the methods of scientific investigation. 2 Vols., 7th ed.* London: Longman, Green, Reader and Dyer. [First published 1843.] https://archive.org/stream/asystemoflogic01milluoft#page/410/mode/2up/search/chemical

——. (1919). *A system of logic, ratiocinative and inductive; being a connected view of the principles of evidence and the methods of scientific investigation*. 8th Ed. [New Impression]. Longmans, Green and Co.

Monier Williams, M. (1899). *A Sanskrit-English Dictionary*. London: Oxford University Press.

Ñāṇamoli. (1997) *The Path of Purification: Visuddhismagga*. Singapore Buddhist Meditation Centre.

Nārada. (1982). *Buddhism in a Nutshell*. Kandy: Buddhist Publication Society. (First published 1933). http://www.buddhanet.net/pdf_file/nutshell.pdf

Neal, Dawn. (2014) The Life and Contributions of CAF Rhys Davids. *The Sati Journal*, 2: 15-31. https://www.academia.edu/11805005/The_Life_and_Contributions_of_CAF_Rhys_Davids

Nyanatiloka (2004). *Buddhist Dictionary*. 4th ed. [1980] Buddhist Publication Society.

Obeyesekere, Gananath. (2002). *Imagining Karma: Ethical Transformation in Amerindian, Buddhist and Greek Rebirth*. University of California Press.

O'Connor, Timothy and Wong, Hong Yu. (2015). Emergent Properties, in *The Stanford Encyclopedia of Philosophy* (Summer 2015 Edition), Edward N. Zalta (ed.). http://plato.stanford.edu/archives/sum2015/entries/properties-emergent

Piya Tan. (2005). '(Anicca) Cakkhu Sutta. The (Impermanent) Eye Discourse.' http://dharmafarer.org/wordpress/wp-content/uploads/2009/12/16.7-Anicca-Cakkhu-S-s25.1-piya.pdf

Pranke, Patrick. (2011). On Saints and Wizards: Ideals of Human Perfection and Power in Contemporary Burmese Buddhism. *Journal of the International Association of Buddhist Studies Volume, 33* (1–2): 453–488. http://nbn-resolving.de/urn:nbn:de:bsz:16-jiabs-92908

Rahula, Walpola. (1974). 'Wrong Notions of *Dhammatā* (*Dharmatā*)', in L. Cousins et al, eds., *Buddhist Studies in Honour of I.B. Horner*, Dordrecht: Reidel, pp.181–91.

Revel, Alex. (1984). *Brief Glory: The Life of Arthur Rhys Davids, DSO, MC & Bar*. William Kimber.

Rhys Davids, C. A. F. (1900). *A Buddhist manual of psychological ethics or Buddhist Psychology, of the Fourth Century B.C.*, being a translation, now made for the first time, from the Original Pāli of the First Book in the Abhidhamma-Piṭaka, entitled Dhamma-Sangaṇi (Compendium of States or Phenomena)

—— (1912). *Buddhism: a Study of the Buddhist Norm*. https://archive.org/stream/MN40132ucmf_6#page/n119/mode/2up

—— (1934). *Buddhism: its birth and dispersal.* (Rev. Ed.). London: Thornton Butterworth Ltd.

Rhys Davids, C. A. F. and Woodward, F. L. (1917–30). *The Book of the Kindred Sayings: or Grouped Suttas*. [5 vols], Pali Text Society.

Robertson, George, Croom. (1896a). Elements of Psychology. Ed. by Rhys Davids, C. A. F. https://archive.org/stream/elementsofpsycho00robeuoft#page/xii/mode/2up

—— (1896b) *Elements of General Philosophy*. Ed. by Rhys Davids, C. A. F. https://archive.org/details/elementsofconstr00robeuoft

Ronkin, Noa. (2005) *Early Buddhist Metaphysics: The Making of a Philosophical Tradition*. Routledge.

Russell, E. S., Morris, C. R., and Mackenzie, W. L. (1926) The Notion of Emergence in *Proceedings of the Aristotelian Society. Supplementary Vol., 6*: 39-68. Reprinted 2014, with an introduction by Goldstein, Jeffery A. in *E:CO 16* (1): 131-168.

Sangharakshita. (1967). *The Three Jewels*. Glasgow: Windhorse.

—— (1973). *Endlessly Fascinating Cry - Part 2*. Unpublished. Available from https://www.freebuddhistaudio.com/texts/seminartexts/SEM063P2_Endlessly_Fascinating_Cry_-_Part_2.pd

—— (1993) *A Survey of Buddhism*. 7th Ed. Glasgow: Windhorse.

—— (1994). *Who Is the Buddha*? Glasgow: Windhorse.

—— (2009). *The Essential Sangharakshita: A Half Century of Writings*. Wisdom Publications.

Sayadaw, Ledi. Ledi Sayadaw. (1965) Niyama-Dipani or Manual of Cosmic Order, in *The Manuals of Buddhism*, trans. Barua, B. M, Rhys Davids, C. A. F., & Nyana. Bangkok: Mahamakut Press, 1978 (orig. publ. 1965). Online at http://mahajana.net/texts/kopia_lokalna/MANUAL04.html

Scharfe, Hartmut . (1999). "The Doctrine of the Three Humors in Traditional Indian Medicine and the Alleged Antiquity of Tamil Siddha Medicine." *Journal of the American Oriental Society* 119(4): 609-629.

Shwe Zan Aung & Rhys Davids, C.A.F. (1915). *Points of Controversy, being a translation of the Kathāvatthu from the Abhidhamma-piṭaka*. London: Pali Text Society.

Smith, John. (2009). *The Mahābhārata*, London: Penguin.

Snodgrass, Judith (2007). "Defining Modern Buddhism: Mr. and Mrs. Rhys Davids and the Pali Text Society." *Comparative Studies of South Asia, Africa and the Middle East.* 27:1, 186-202. http://muse.jhu.edu/journals/cst/summary/v027/27.1snodgrass.html.

Subhuti. (2010). *Revering and Relying Upon the Dharma: Sangharakshita's approach to Right View*. 1st Published in Shabda. July, 2010.

—— (2012). "A Supra-personal Force or Energy Working Through Me: the Triratna Buddhist Community and the Stream of the Dharma". http://www.subhuti.info/sites/subhuti.info/files/pdf/A-Supra-Personal-Force.pdf

Thanissaro. (2005) *Trans. Sivaka Sutta: To Sivaka* [SN 36.21]. *Access to Insight*. http://www.accesstoinsight.org/tipitaka/sn/sn36/sn36.021.than.html

Tripāṭhī, C. (1962). *Fünfundzwanzig Sūtras des Nidānasaṃyukta.* (Sanskrittexte aus den Turfanfunden, VIII). Berlin : Akademie-Verlag. Online at GRETIL.

Yin Shun. (1983*) Combined Edition of Sūtra and Śāstra of the Saṃyuktāgama.* Shanghai: Zhonghua Book Company. [印順. (1983) 雜阿含經論會編. 中華書局.]

Jayarava has been a member of the Triratna Buddhist Order since 2005. His scholarship has appeared in the *Journal of Buddhist Ethics*, the *Journal of the Oxford Centre for Buddhist Studies*, *Contemporary Buddhism*, and the *Journal of Chinese Buddhist Studies*. He has become a world expert on the history and interpretation of the *Heart Sutra* and recently published a major study of the history of the Buddhist ideas of karma and rebirth. Since 2002 Jayarava has lived in Cambridge, UK.

www.ingramcontent.com/pod-product-compliance
Lightning Source LLC
Chambersburg PA
CBHW071611040426
42452CB00008B/1313
9780956692931